Knitting

Heaven

and

Earth

BROADWAY BOOKS

NEW YORK

Knitting Heaven and Earth

HEALING

the HEART

with CRAFT

Susan Gordon Lydon

PRINTED IN THE UNITED STATES OF AMERICA

BROADWAY BOOKS and its logo, a letter B bisected on the
diagonal, are trademarks of Random House, Inc.

Visit our Web site at www.broadwaybooks.com

First edition published 2005

Book design by Maria Carella
Photo on title page courtesy of Corbis royalty-free images

Library of Congress Cataloging-in-Publication Data
Lydon, Susan Gordon, 1943-
    Knitting heaven and earth : healing the heart with craft /
Susan Gordon Lydon.
        p. cm.
    ISBN 0-7679-1565-8
    1. Knitting—Philosophy. 2. Lydon, Susan Gordon, 1943- I. Title.
TT820.L92   2005
746.43'2—dc22   2004061781

10   9   8   7   6   5   4   3   2   1

FOR

Linda Mellon Ratto

and

Marilyn Gross Rinzler

Contents

Acknowledgments

WITH GRATEFUL THANKS TO SHARON DYNAK AND THE Ucross Foundation for giving me a place where my imagination could roam free; to Anne Merrow, Mary Peacock, and Beth Haymaker for their heroic efforts on behalf of this manuscript; and to my intrepid agent, Susan Raihofer, who never let me rest until I had completed the proposal for this book.

Oakland, California
July 2004

Once in a while, you get shown the light
In the strangest of places, if you look at it right.

"Scarlet Begonias"
(Robert Hunter/Jerry Garcia)
Grateful Dead
From the Mars Hotel

Introduction:
Womb to Tomb
Knitting

YEARS AGO, IN THE LATE 1970S, I PUBLISHED A NEWSPA-
per out of my apartment in New York City. I called
its parent company Womb to Tomb Publishing, not
without irony. Now it seems like what I do is Womb
to Tomb Knitting. Knitting has become my deepest
means of expressing the love I feel for people in my
life, my way of connecting to their spirits and hearts,
my way of helping them in and out of this world.

When my niece Maggie was trying to carry a
baby to term after repeatedly miscarrying, I knitted to
hold her baby fast to earth. Not that I can claim
credit for the miracles of birth, but Maggie is now
raising three healthy children in Australia. When my
friend Linda Cross lay dying of non-Hodgkins lymphoma and I was unable to get to Boston to see her,

I knitted her a hat of the softest, most sumptuous black cashmere to comfort her. I knew I had fallen in love with my godson, Ishi, before he was even born when I began the first baby sweater I had knitted in thirty years.

I set out to write a book about various types of love: familial love, parental love, romantic love. But the events of my life intervened, and I had to go, as my spiritual teacher, Oscar Ichazo, describes it, "deepier and deepier." (I have been studying with Oscar Ichazo in the Arica Institute, a mystical school of meditation and metaphysics, a university without walls, since 1973.)

Soon I was submerged in matters of death, illness, sorrow, and loss. Then this story became about a different sort of love, as I discovered the enormous power handcrafts possess to heal and integrate us as we confront the major calamities of life. The simple practices of handknitting and needlepoint have enabled me to journey within myself, to explore the mysteries of my own heart and my connections with others, to find the relationship with my true self that empowers me to live from my core. Handcrafts have served as my path to enlightenment, the vehicle for my shamanic journey, the way I discover who I am and make progress toward knowing how to care for myself as well as for others, my consolation in times of unbearable stress.

I used to say I was writing a book about knitting and love. Then, when it changed direction, I started calling it a book about knitting and death. "Knitting and death," my friend Lyle Poncher said when I told him. "I like it. It's catchy."

The time frame covered by the events in this book is roughly 1995-2004. Part of the story concerns an exploration of what love is and isn't. It follows the trajectory of a failed romantic relationship, a redeemed relationship with a parent, a joyful bond with a child who came into my life by choice. All these connections opened my heart and expanded my capacity for love, whether by shattering my heart into a million pieces, causing it to dance for joy, or bringing it peace by putting the past to rest.

Sorrow and grief are the price we pay for loving others, for forming attachments to our fellow mortals in a transitory life on Planet Earth. We live inside human bodies that are frangible, easily injured, prone to illness and ultimate disappearance, what the swamis call deincarnation. What gives us the strength to face these losses, to keep putting one foot in front of the other and continue our earth walk while we are here? All of us must find answers to these questions.

Through the story I tell here, fragmented and episodic as it occurred in actual life, I knitted and stitched. When I attended my father at his deathbed, knitting enabled me to sit still and pay attention. Knitting expanded time into a kind of spaciousness, allowing me to be present at occasions from which I would rather have escaped. What I lived informed my knitting, and what I learned from knitting informed my life.

When I wrote my previous book, *The Knitting Sutra*, I was following a thread, as it were, that presented itself to me in the form of my most compelling impulses and enduring desires. I had a hunch that this seemingly simple and inscrutable activity that had brought me so much pleasure and wisdom and sustained generations of women before me might have far more to it than met the eye. What I found in writing the book was that the practice of handcraft, and the journey toward mastery of craft, had provided women with profound spiritual nourishment that had for the most part remained a secret part of their inner lives.

The readers and knitters who came to my readings and workshops were intensely appreciative that someone had understood and put into words what they had felt and experienced in pursuing their craft. Over the years that the book has been in print, I've been following this thread further as it has manifested itself in the events of my own life, in the insights it has presented to me as I worked, in the practice of knitting after I mastered its basics. I continue to think of knitting as a metaphor for the inner journey, as well as a productive activity in its own right, and of course as my guiding passion.

As I write this, knitting is enjoying a "moment," as a full-fledged cultural trend. Some of the young men and women learning to knit now, fashioning scarves out of thick yarn on big needles, may become what Meg Swansen calls true knitters. Some may discover knitting as a boon to their inner selves. Some may abandon it and go on to the next cultural trend. Myself, I continue on the journey that began for me with *The Knitting Sutra*.

As the epigraph to *Howards End*, E. M. Forster wrote, "Only connect." Knitting connects. It connects us to one another. It connects us to our deepest selves, to the vastness of our ancestral knowledge and internal landscape. It connects us to the elemental forces of the universe, the pull of gravity, the solidity of earth, the majestic roll and swell of the oceans, to weather and wind, the animal, bird, and vegetable life around us, the ethereal heavenly spheres where our inspiration flourishes. Humble though it is, I believe knitting has within it the power to connect heaven with earth. And according to the *I Ching*, or the Chinese *Book of Changes*, when heaven and earth unite, what happens is a profound and enduring peace.

1. Animal Comfort

FOR ABOUT TEN YEARS I'VE BEEN GOING TO THE RUSsian River resort area in Northern California at the end of July with my friend Lou and her family. We stay at a place called Summerhome Park, situated at a bend in the green, snaky river. Hills of redwood trees rise from its banks, and the air, carrying the combined fragrances of redwood, bay, and running river water, is so fresh and clean you wish you could bottle it and bring it home.

I sleep in the cabin with Lou's sister-in-law, Tina, and over the years a small group of what I've come to call cranky middle-aged women have emerged as a core of regular yearly guests. Besides Lou, who's been my closest friend for over a decade, and me, the group includes Tina and her longtime friend Theresa, both of them labor and delivery nurses.

Each year I watch the passage and progress of an osprey or a family of ospreys that appears precisely around the bend in the river each morning and late afternoon to fish. It announces its presence with a distinctive whistle my father taught me to recognize on one of our bird-watching trips to the Everglades and is always an exhilarating sight. I once observed the parent ospreys taking their fledgling children on a trial flight, leading them on with a fish skeleton one parent held in its mouth.

Summerhome Park is one of those resorts built in the 1920s or 1930s, when wealthy families from San Francisco went to the Russian River to summer. It is an idyllic place for children, woodsy and mysterious, with a wide, safe beach, a lodge where teenagers can hang out, buying candy and hamburgers and shooting pool, and many secluded spots along the river for canoeing, fishing, and Huck Finn-type imaginative wilderness adventures.

While the kids are hanging out at the lodge or around campfires on the beach, we women play a card game called Spite and Malice. It is a complicated form of multihanded solitaire. I'm sure Spite and Malice got its name from the viciously competitive way it must be played. The game's objective is to get rid of your pile of cards before anyone else does, and one way of doing it is by purposely blocking your opponents' progress. Since Tina learned it from an elderly woman she helps care for named Lucille, we call our game Lucille.

In the long, lazy evenings after dinner at the river, we women play many games of Lucille. I am a bridge player and can endure almost anything with good games of cards. I used to say that the best thing about being in jail was that there were always enough people to play cards with, and in the course of many stays in rehab, I survived by playing spades, a simpler form of bridge, with my fellows. When I was a child on Long Island, and hurricanes or thunderstorms knocked out our power and flooded the only bridge to town, my father would light candles and play leisurely games of canasta or Steal the Old Man's Bundle with the kids.

Theresa came to Summerhome Park as a child. Her aunt and uncle owned a small general and grocery store she helped out in. It had long been boarded up, though still scenic, when we discovered Summerhome Park and began to go there.

I don't know that Tina, who is goodhearted and generous almost to a fault, would describe herself as cranky. But Theresa's eccentricities would make her embrace the description wholeheartedly. Together, the four of us generate a powerful female energy that reminds me of matriarchs in an elephant or buffalo herd. I once saw a buffalo cow give birth in Golden Gate Park. The other females surrounded her in a circle of protection. That is the sort of energy we possess.

Of course I bring my knitting to the river. One year I was experimenting with luxury materials. I had begun to knit with a fiber known as qiviut that had recently come onto the commercial market. Qiviut is spun from the downy underhair of the musk ox, a shaggy Arctic beast that roams the frozen tundra and puts one in mind of a smaller, stubbier version of the woolly mammoth.

The animal is little changed from the Ice Age. According to an article by Donna Druchunas in the Fall 2003 issue of *Interweave Knits*, the musk ox, which was hunted nearly to extinction in the 1860s, lives in remote areas of Greenland, Alaska, and Canada, "where it grows an underwool that is…eight times warmer than sheep's wool. This layer of qiviut protects the animals in −100° F weather; in fact, captive herds must be protected from overheating when temperatures rise to just 70° F."

To the Yupiit people of Alaska, the animal is known as the oomingmak ("the bearded one"). And qiviut, the yarn spun from its soft, downy underfleece, is said to be finer, warmer, and lighter than cashmere. "With each animal producing just five to seven pounds of qiviut each year," Druchunas writes, "the fiber remains rare and expensive." There are cooperatives of Inuit women in the Yukon who make garments from qiviut and sell them by mail order. They are costly and exquisite. But the fiber became available for the home knitter only in the past decade, when a woman named Nancy Bender began raising musk oxen on a farm in Hamilton, Montana, and having the underfleece spun into yarn.

At about the same time, a company somewhere began producing luxurious knitting needles made of rosewood and ebony. I bought a pair of ebony straight needles with rosewood knobs and imagined myself knitting qiviut on ebony in the very height of luxury.

The needles didn't work out too well for me; the wood was hard and hurt my hands. But the qiviut worked out fine.

It was at that time available only in taupe brown, the natural color of the fleece, a color that seemed as though it would be comforting in a cozy animal way. Warmth for weight ratio is a big deal in the fiber world. Mohair, for instance, has a very high degree of warmth for its light weight, and cashmere has been coveted for years because of this quality. Of course not all cashmere is created equal. The diet of the goats, the altitude at which they are raised, the processing of the fleece, and the spinning, as well as the raw fleece itself, make the feel of the fiber vary widely.

Downy fibers such as qiviut and cashmere possess what is called a halo, the fine hairs that surround the core of spun fiber and make it more or less fuzzy depending on the yarn. They are also said to bloom with washing. As the fiber absorbs water and the tightness of the spin relaxes, the yarn fluffs up and softens in an appealing way. This works particularly well with lace patterns, as the halo blooms and occupies the empty spaces formed by the yarnovers or holes in the lace.

By this point I had been knitting so much and so passionately that I had caught up with most new developments in the knitting world, had become current, as it were, and was hungry for novelty and variety.

I found in a book of classic British Isles knitwear a pattern for a lace shawl that was pictured wrapped around a baby. It didn't look very large. I ordered a couple of skeins of qiviut from Nancy Bender and began knitting my first lacy shawl. Did I mention that the yarn was extravagantly pricey? It made cashmere look like a bargain.

The shawl was in the pattern known as feather and fan, or old shale, which makes a scallopy edge to the design. Though it was not the first time I knitted lace, it was the first of many shawls I was to knit and started me on a major binge of lace shawl knitting. This piece had a simple triangular shape rather than the large squares I later made, and it featured only one lace pattern rather than the varying patterns of the others.

Who knows why one pattern feels so pleasurable and comfortable to knit while another feels frustrating and irritating? This for me is one of the enduring mysteries of lace knitting. But the rhythm and feel of the feather and fan appealed to me right from the start. I loved the rhythm of its yarnovers and decreases, the mathematical arabesque of adding and subtracting stitches, the alternating columns and arches that appeared with each repetition of the pattern.

But the quantity of yarn required for the piece had not been precisely delineated in the instructions, and its finished size had been concealed in the folds wrapped around the baby. So I kept running out of yarn. Every week it seemed I was calling Nancy Bender to tell her I needed more qiviut while the price for the project mounted ever upward. Also, since the fleece had been gathered from different animals and was available only in its natural color, the skeins did not match exactly in color, weight, or finish of thread. Some were lighter in color, some darker, some smoother, some fluffier, with a shaggier feel more like mohair.

I was about midway through the shawl when I went to the Russian River that year, in 1997, and the price of the yarn had already soared to about $250, with no end in sight.

Theresa pulled it right out of my knitting bag. "What is this?" she demanded as the shawl fluffed up into its shaggy, lacy animal beauty. "I want this," she said. "I have to have it."

"I can't possibly sell it for what the materials cost," I said. "The yarn has already cost two hundred fifty dollars, and I'm nowhere near finished."

"I would pay you five or six hundred dollars for something like this," she said. Theresa lives near the ocean in San Diego. Both her husband and her daughter are avid surfers. She was already imagining the comforting fluffy shawl wrapped around her shoulders on chilly evenings at the beach.

When it was finished, I sold it to her. To my exacting knitter's eye, the shawl was far from perfect. There were mistakes in the lace, so the columns and arches didn't line up precisely. The color wasn't uniform, as it would be if one were to buy all the yarn at one time, in the same dye lot. It varied from light to dark, from finer to thicker, from smooth to furry in various parts.

The shape was asymmetrical, and the size somewhere between a shawl and a scarf, not the generous enveloping wrap I'm sure Theresa had imagined. I hadn't yet learned how to block lace, so it was lumpy and bumpy. It possessed plenty of that quality the Japanese call *wabi sabi*, the charm of the imperfect.

But Theresa didn't think so.

"I don't know what I ever did to deserve anything as beautiful as this," she said, "but it must have been good."

In truth the shawl was cozy and comforting, not so very far from the animals that had given their downy underhair to create the yarn, and of course it had absorbed all that female energy that the four of us, plus Tina's other nurse friends, generated on the river.

It was also the first time I was ever paid what I thought was a fair price for my labor and materials.

Theresa loved it. She kept it in a special box. Enshrined, she said, like the relic of a saint. And since she, Tina, and Lou all had grown up in Roman Catholic families, Theresa thought of a singularly Catholic use for the shawl.

"This is the sort of thing," she said, "that I want to be wearing in my open casket."

"I never would have thought of that," I said, "but now that you mention it, it seems fine."

Over the years we've been going to the Russian River all of us have lost members of our families. Lou has lost a brother; Tina's lost both parents and two brothers; Theresa's brother and my father have died. Though we are together for only a short, intense time each year, we have used our connection and companionship to mourn and console, to comfort and succor one another. We have shared the deaths in our families that have occurred between each season.

Theresa, who is from a large Mexican family, liked to regale us with stories about her late brother Louie, who had been something of an outlaw and reprobate. He rode a Harley, trafficked in illicit substances, and had a large number of girlfriends who streamed through the house in a steady procession as he lay dying upstairs of liver disease.

"Louie's fools," Theresa called them. According to her, the women remained devoted to Louie even though she did everything in her power to dissuade them. "You don't want to go up there," she would tell one of them. "Mary is already there, and you know how much you hate her."

"I couldn't really blame them," Theresa said, "because Louie was so appealing. But I'm glad I was his sister, so I didn't have to be one of his fools."

The women mourned en masse at Louie's funeral, a colorful affair that naturally featured the deceased in an open casket. Some of Louie's buddies had thoughtfully provided him with some sustenance for the afterlife, several joints of marijuana placed in the breast pocket of his shirt.

Theresa marched right up to the casket and took the joints out of Louie's pocket, "because," as she said, "he wouldn't be needing them where he was going, and I needed them right then."

Theresa and Tina saw each other between times at the river, and Lou and I lived close to each other at home, but the four of us rarely gathered except at the river. One winter Lou went with Tina to San Diego, and Theresa conducted what she called a showing of the shawl in its special box.

Tina's mother had been ill and on dialysis for some time, but when she died suddenly, Tina was devastated. Theresa wasn't able to attend the funeral, but she offered Tina what, to her mind, was the next best consolation to her presence.

"I told her I was sorry I couldn't come to the funeral," she said. "But I said she could borrow the shawl to wear."

She called it the shawl as though it were the only one in the world and everyone would know what she meant. As though it possessed magical powers. As though it could function as an intermediary between worlds, between animals and humans, between the living and the dead.

For Tina and Theresa, who were so often present at the mysteries of birth, the occasions of birth and death required a kind of animal comfort. The swaddling of the baby. The shrouding of the corpse. The wearing of a magic shawl to ease the pain of grief. All these times demanded a kind of bundling or wrapping that would somehow aid the body's passage between the states of being and nonbeing.

A shawl is a garment to be wrapped around the wearer. It envelops the person in warmth. It is a natural project for the contemplative nature of knitting. Prayer shawl ministries have now sprung up in many areas of the country. They are groups that knit for members in distress, stitching their work with prayer and positive intention. Then they wrap the recipients in the shawls as a blessing.

The last time I saw Theresa, she told me she had loaned the qiviut shawl to her mother. Her mother suffers from lymphoma, and Theresa thought the shawl might ease the pain of the tumors in her neck.

Theresa's mother is something of a fancy lady. According to Theresa, she never goes out even to do her gardening in anything but nylon hose and immaculate Ferragamos. Now she has a shaggy, imperfect, hand-stitched shawl to warm the achings of her heart and her neck. And since the shawl has a life of its own, like a child you've given birth to, she will probably never know it comes to her courtesy of the great, shambling Arctic beasts whose coats provided the yarn, and of the nimble fingers of the knitter that was me.

2. Knitting on the Wing

AS I WRITE THESE WORDS, IN 2003, IT HAS BEEN TWELVE years since I broke my right arm and my orthopedist told me to exercise the small muscles of my hands to keep them from atrophying as the bone healed. I rediscovered knitting in that time and determined to go farther than I ever had, to transform myself from a mediocre to a master knitter.

To a large extent, I have accomplished what I set out to do. I mastered two-handed Fair Isle knitting along with every sort of cable and embossed pattern and discovered that I did not want to do intarsia knitting and loved knitting lace with a passion.

I've been knitting virtually nonstop for the past twelve years. I thought that knitting had no end, no bottom and that it could sustain me for a lifetime, but I am beginning to wonder: What do you do with knitting once you've achieved mastery of its techniques?

Barbara Walker, who wrote the four *Treasury of Knitting Patterns* series and did as much as anyone to popularize handknitting in the United States, eventually discovered that what she loved was mosaic knitting, but that she no longer desired to make full-size garments. Instead she began making knitted clothes for dolls.

In my own case, I have gotten to know myself better, refined the details of what I knew, and explored the limits of what knitting could and could not do in my life.

I have always liked to make clothes and been fascinated with tailoring. My ancestors were furriers and tailors, and I had a feel for sewing in my genes. In my childhood I owned a leopard-skin coat my grandfather made for me. It was Somali leopard, not yet endangered or forbidden. My grandfather had a piece left over after making my aunt Blanche a grownup coat in a 1940s style. I was a tactile child, and I liked to feel the short, bristly hairs that lay smoothly over the pelt of the fur. My grandfather also gave me mink tails and scraps of silk lining to play with; my mother and I fashioned them into doll clothes. I loved the feel of the fur tails and the red silk satin we combined into a coat.

After I had mastered the basics of what I wanted to know in knitting, my tailoring genes took over, and I began to experiment with refining the details and fit of the jacket sweater that I knitted, with variations of course, again and again.

For instance, the setting in of a sleeve at the shoulder and the underarm is of supreme importance to the look of a garment. In my opinion, shoulder construction is what makes a jacket by the Italian designer Giorgio Armani look so elegant and flattering to the wearer.

I have read there are ateliers in Naples, reportedly the center of fine Italian tailoring, where you have to work for twenty-five years, learning all other aspects of construction, before you are allowed to set a sleeve into a jacket.

The French designer Sonia Rykiel is also good at armhole construction in sweaters. Her armholes tend to be high and tight, but though they give a good look to the sweater, they are really not suitable for an overgarment, such as a jacket or cardigan.

After many years I reached the point where I knitted so much that I could afford the luxury of making an entire garment just to experiment with a different shoulder, neckline, length, or armhole. I was not particularly attached to the end result of wearing one of these garments. I thought of them instead as art projects and of the yarn I used in their construction as art supplies.

I like the look of plain stockinette, knit on the right side, purl on the wrong side. For wearing, I tend to prefer fine yarn in plain dark colors, but that is not necessarily what I like to knit. I have discovered over time that my preferred needle size is between a four and an eight. Smaller and larger needles tend to hurt my hands, though I often use larger needles if I've fallen in love with a yarn that requires them. And lately I'm so impatient with my projects that every other thing I do is knit on size elevens.

I have experimented with making the armholes of my sweater

jackets as tight and as loose as I could, resulting in everything from a classic set-in sleeve to a modified drop shoulder. I've also tried different sorts of necklines. I made an entire black wool sweater, with hefty cables, just to see how the folded-over crew neck would look.

Over the years I became adept at fit. I could knit a sweater to my own or someone else's measurements, though variations in how different yarns behave still make this a chancy undertaking. I could pretty much make something look the way I wanted it to. I learned what looked good on me and what would never look good on me. I discovered that no matter what or how well I knitted, I was not going to look like Cindy Crawford or Kate Moss in the end.

As I wrote in *The Knitting Sutra*, you'd be surprised at how many years it took me to figure this out.

I gave myself a lot of permission to let my creativity flourish freely in my knitting. Although I often sold my finished projects, I never took on commissions. I wanted to be able to abandon a project if it began to bore me, if I made some hideous mistake, or if the yarn simply did not want to become what I was trying to force it into. "Life is too short to knit what you don't like," I thought, just as I no longer forced myself to finish books I didn't much care for.

There are knitters who put a lot of restrictions on their knitting lives. They work on only one project at a time; they make sure it has a practical purpose; they are careful not to spend too much money on materials.

There are probably as many types of knitters as there are stitch patterns for knitting, but I am not of the puritanical mind-set that believes in limiting pleasure in my creative life. The structural constrictions of making a three-dimensional garment from a flat piece of thread are limitation enough as far as I'm concerned.

So I indulge every whim, spend any amount of money to get the yarn I want, let the knitter within get away with murder, metaphorically speaking. I abandon projects in midstream, experiment freely, do what I want, when I want, and hang the consequences. I want the knitter in me to be as free, wild, artistic, and creative as she has the desire to be. Knitting is where I give the wild woman inside me free rein. If she wants to be the wise woman as well, that's fine; if not, also fine. I no longer care that my kitchen cupboards are stuffed with yarn, and my closets with half-finished projects.

I knit with cashmere often because it is kind to my hands, which have endured bouts of tendinitis on and off for years.

At this point in my life I say: Judge me if you dare.

————

It took me years of being a writer before I discovered and could accept my own particular rhythms and needs for that creative process. I don't write every day, never have, and have rarely followed a routine, yet no one can tell me I am not a writer because I don't follow some other person's formula for what a writer does.

It took a shorter time for me to work out what sort of knitter I was and wasn't. I like rhythmic knitting, and that is why intarsia, the knitting of a picture inlaid into the fabric, is not for me. Intarsia, which produces beautiful results, beloved by many knitters, is more like weaving or embroidery. You have to stop to change colors, anchor them into the fabric, knit in the edges formed while you work. The same process is required in making one of those Kaffe Fassett coats of many textures and many colors. Being a stop-and-start sort of affair, intarsia lacks the comforting rhythmic quality of stockinette or jacquard pattern-on-pattern knitting. Not my cup of tea.

————————

I know highly experienced knitters whom I think of as construction innovators. They will do almost anything to avoid the back, front, two sleeves construction of a sweater. Lisa Daniels of Big Sky Luxury Yarns in Lafayette, California, is this sort of knitter. She likes to start, say, in the middle of the front and knit out toward the sides or with a diagonal construction that begins at one corner and increases and decreases at both sides to form an eventual rectangle.

Lisa loves to mix colors and textures. She is a flamboyant dresser and a wildly extravagant colorist, and she's been at her craft so long that she's discovered what she needs to maintain her interest.

"I knew exactly what kind of knitter you were when you walked in the store," she said to me one day. Sure enough, I had a lacy shawl in my knitting bag. "A detail knitter. You're like my mother, an executer rather than an innovator."

That was fair. Though I rarely make a pattern without modifying it or combining elements with other patterns, I don't think of myself as a designer. Lisa guessed my proclivities so well that the last time I went into Big Sky, she simply led me to the buttery cashmere and put three balls of brilliant turquoise into a bag. She knew that once I got acquainted with the yarn, plunging my hands into its plush depths and admiring its vibrant color, I would have no choice but to take it home.

————————

Jacqueline Olsen of Amazing Threads is another construction innovator. I made her Tea Trader's Tunic, which I bought by mail order, and spoke to her on the phone. Olsen has been a professional knitwear designer for years and years. Her daughter draws the lovely pencil illustrations that make her patterns so alluring to the eye.

The Tea Trader's Tunic was made of a tomato red cotton blend. The finish of the thread was flat enough to show stitches to advantage. The tunic was trimmed with a deep border in a twill stitch that formed itself into a dramatic diagonal point at the back. The front had an asymmetrical Chinese closing with a mandarin collar of the twill.

Olsen later told me that she had originally designed the tunic with a set-in sleeve, which I would have preferred, but simplified it for mass marketing. I rarely wear the Tea Trader's Tunic but will always be happy that I found a way to make it.

————————

While I can appreciate the art involved in formulating these unusual and imaginative constructions, I have a difficult body to fit and so prefer to make my pieces one at a time in order to adjust measurements and ensure proper sizing. I like to choose a beautiful color that I know I will continue to enjoy through the completion of an entire project, and to make the knitting interesting with pattern, texture, and sometimes style.

Although I love the look of plain stockinette knitting, too much doing of it bores me to tears. My friend Debbie Kolb, who taught me to knit in college, mostly knits large projects in stockinette on small needles because she likes to knit while reading or at the movies. I like just enough pattern or texture that I have to pay attention. Though I have done some knitting that is so demanding and intricate it can only be performed when I'm at home alone, with no distractions or interruptions, I almost always take my knitting on the road.

For the past several years I've knitted a lot of lace, making fine shawls that need no fitting but require a lot of attention to detail. In order to knit lace, you need a row counter, and you need to keep meticulous count of stitches and rows. I sometimes teach beginning lace students to count their stitches after each row to make sure they haven't inadvertently added an extra yarnover or decreased one time too many. The counting and rhythms of knitting lace, though soothing and productive, are also exacting, and unless you knit a lace pattern that has become second nature to you, it is essential to pay close attention to what you are doing as you knit.

In recent years I've been inspired by the beautifully hand-painted yarns that emerge from the dye pots of several interesting designers. Colinette Sainsbury of Wales is one of the pioneers of artful dyeing, in which yarns are not submerged in a bath of solid color but are painted with dyes to achieve delicate shadings that produce uneven, colorful, and unexpected effects when you knit with them. I think of working with these yarns as Adventures in Dye Lots. As with my lacy qiviut shawl, you never know quite what you're going to end up with when you begin a project with hand-painted yarns.

I first saw the Koigu painters' palette merino yarns at the Yarnery in St. Paul, Minnesota, one of my favorite yarn shops. I bought them in a number of colors and staggered them in a shawl pattern called Charlotte's Web. I haven't stopped knitting with Koigu since.

I experimented with Schaefer yarns, which are also beautifully dyed, after making a number of one-skein baby sweaters out of Elaine, a thick and thin, bulky, soft merino yarn. I began my own sorts of improvisations. With dye lots that are impossible to duplicate, one sometimes obtains surprising results, such as a single color bunching up into a solid block, or colors forming horizontal stripes, when knitting with these yarns. I designed a sweater made of different shades of Elaine right on my needles as I went along.

Claudia Hoffberg, a spinner and dyer, has a shop called Deep Color not far from my house. The yarn she spins and dyes by hand is bulky yet light; it has a lot of air spun into it and, as she says, "a lot of hand." I also designed a jacket in various colors of Claudia's yarn, framed in shades of indigo, on my needles, improvising as I went. In color work, it is always compelling to see how the next shade will change the look of the whole. I finished the jacket with silver concho buttons I had bought in Gallup, New Mexico, many years before. Large and sterling silver, they make a pleasing noise. They ring, as the expression goes, with the sound of silver on the bar.

Though I myself don't spin or dye, one quality I've come to appreciate in this hand-spun, hand-dyed yarn is what's known as abrash, an uneven saturation of color one often sees in oriental or Navajo rugs. I like the shaded colors, unexpected effects, and unmistakable handmade look of the soft vegetal tones.

For years I've been trying to knit the ideal sweater, Plato's sweater, the comfortable, slouchy garment you'd grab off the chair every time you went out of the house. By ideal I don't mean perfected, just the idea of a quest, a pursuit of a chimera, a vision that you hold in your mind as you go. I don't know that I'll ever attain this ideal, but I do know that it keeps me knitting.

Most of the time my results fall short of perfection, but perfection is not what I'm aiming for in my experiments. Sometimes I'm just trying to sustain and amuse myself. Often I try to let the material dictate the design of a garment rather than force it into a preordained pattern where it has no business being. Sometimes a piece of knitting is simply itself.

I've also fooled around with transforming materials after a garment has been finished. Over the years my hands have become adept at many things but, most of all, at blocking, the shaping of pieces for finishing. "Strong knitter's hands," a physical therapist said when she took my hands to test my grip. My hands have smoothed and patted lace into position until it is flat and the pattern shines through, have made various pieces of sweaters bigger or smaller, softened some materials and roughed up others to make the nap come alive. I've soaked sweaters in lavender laundry water, hair conditioner, olive oil, and lanolin, shrunk them in hot water and stretched them in cold, poured on humectants to make wool less itchy, and fluffed up cotton in a hot dryer, never quite knowing what will turn out in the end.

I haven't yet experimented with felting, though I know it's currently popular. That's not to say that I won't felt at some future time, just for the thrill of transforming a finished knitted garment into something completely different, a warmer, softer, smaller version of itself.

———

In the Shetland Islands, lace shawls are stretched, or dressed, on large wooden frames that have nails pounded into them at regular intervals. After the shawl has been soaked in water, the finisher catches the points of the sawtooth border with thread and attaches these to the nails. The stretched-out shawl is then put outside to dry. Fair Isle sweaters are stretched on woolly boards, or crude representations of the human form. So effective are these for smoothing the multicolored knitting that no knitter can win a Fair Isle competition without using one of these contraptions.

One pattern I've made over and over is the Kerry Blue Shawl from Martha Waterman's book *Traditional Knitted Lace Shawls*. When I began knitting the first one, which I'll talk about later in the book, my boyfriend offered to make me a frame. It didn't quite work out. I then went to Lacis, a store in Berkeley run by the late Kaethe Kliot, an expert on Old World construction and all sorts of lace, who suggested that I block the shawl on my mattress. My first shawl attempts had sewn-on borders, which often tore and had to be repaired when I stretched the shawl big enough to be smooth. But a woman who came to one of my knitting retreats at the Esalen Institute, on the spectacular Big Sur coast, showed me how to knit the border directly onto the shawl; this vastly improved the smoothness and drape of the finished product.

Lace must be blocked to bring out its full beauty. When you knit it, it is bumpy and uneven, and you would never know until the finishing how pristine and lovely it can look. The blocking and dressing are immensely satisfying because they complete the transformation from thread to finished garment.

———

Another of my great enthusiasms in knitting, sometimes as important as the choice of fiber, is the buttons. I derive a great deal of pleasure from matching the yarns of my sweaters to suitable buttons. I love buttons made of beautiful woods, or sterling silver, or abalone shell, carved and dyed shells of various kinds. I like to use the sorts of buttons that match the color so precisely that they disappear into the garment or that are so striking they call attention to themselves and eclipse the sweater.

I've been known to make whole sweaters to match buttons I've obtained. Once, at the annual Stitches Market put on by *Knitter's Magazine* (of which more later), I bought some handblown Venetian glass buttons. They had smeary spots of red, blue, yellow, and white, pressed into the tiny millefiori swirls of Murano glass. I couldn't resist them and then had to invent a sweater to showcase their beauty.

Another time I gave a reading at Artfibers in San Francisco. With the gift certificate I received, I chose some antique buttons with delicate abalone flowers inlaid in a background of vintage black plastic. To go with them, I constructed a businesslike black jacket knit from one thin strand of rayon and a slightly thicker rayon bouclé held together. The finished fabric was firm and richly textured, and the jacket meticulously tailored. The buttons shone like gold.

———

I've spent more money on luxury fibers or magnificent buttons for my knitting than I have on finished whole garments for my wardrobe. I've experimented with all sorts of cashmere yarns, from cones of pashmina (which refers to cashmere from India) sold by mail order from Joseph Galler, to hand-spun cashmere from goats raised at an altitude in Colorado similar to the Russian climate where they thrive, to small skeins of hand-painted cashmere from Mountain Colors in Montana. I think of my willingness to use the best materials available as a way to value my talent and my time.

I have allowed myself in my knitting every liberty, every indulgence, every aspect that would make it an activity of pure pleasure and enjoyment rather than of obligation or work. And though the results of my knitting are sometimes practical, artistic self-expression rather than practicality is my primary goal.

While I am not a particularly original or even accomplished knitter, I am an impassioned knitter. I cannot say that my approach would work for anyone else. It works for me. It has kept me inspired and happy. Though it hasn't been good for my pocketbook, it has been good for my spirit, soothing to my troubled mind. It has grounded me in times of happiness and consoled me through times of illness, sorrow, and loss.

Knitting has given my soul a way to fly free. I owe to the humble practice of knitting more than I can ever say.

3. Possessing the Secret of Happiness

I ASSOCIATE KNITTING WITH SOME OF THE HAPPIEST times in my life as well as some of the saddest. In 1967, when I was pregnant with my daughter, Shuna, I was overcome by a sudden desire to knit. I started to knit her a single tiny baby sweater. But knitting, as it has so many times in my life, grew like Topsy until it overtook everything else. Soon I became consumed with it, and multiple projects were scattered around my house.

In the latter months of my pregnancy I sat in the living room of my San Francisco flat listening to music and knitting. There were two records I played over and over. One was the Mozart concerto later used as the theme for the movie *Elvira Madigan*. The other was Bob Dylan's *Highway 61 Revisited*.

What was it about that record that I found so compelling? Everything, I suppose. The ragged guitar chords. The pounding rhythms. The evocative lyrics, resonant with feeling. "Won't you come see me, Queen Jane!" It formed the backdrop for this period of my life, during the late 1960s, in which I was very happy and content.

I would describe the feeling I experienced as sinking down into a state of grace and retreating into the richness of the inner life. I had a task that was of the utmost importance and could not be hurried—in this case, growing a baby to term—and I threw myself into it and wanted for nothing.

Lately when I think of this time, more than thirty-five years ago, I wonder: Was I knitting because I was happy or happy because I was knitting? I did not knit another baby sweater for another three decades, and that was under entirely different circumstances.

I believe I was knitting my daughter's passage into the world. I had already lost one child and was restrained from a full-hearted joy with this pregnancy because of my awareness of its possible perils. I remembered that what had pulled me out of terrible grief after I gave birth to my stillborn baby was reading Dickens's *Pickwick Papers* and knitting a sweater for my husband out of yarn I bought at Jaeger in London. In the years since then, I've read other accounts of women knitting to ease their grief over the deaths of children. In these accounts, most recently by the writer Ann Hood, the women say that knitting sustained them and gave them the courage to move forward with their lives.

By far my strangest knitting-for-the-baby experience was with my godson, Ishi. In 1994 I had surgery for kidney cancer. Following the nephrectomy, I stayed at home, taking it easy for several weeks. The first social event I attended was a birthday party for a young woman I didn't know. She was hugely pregnant and clearly uncomfortable. I didn't make much contact with her. I was not consciously aware that *any* contact had been made. But I began knitting a baby sweater, my first in thirty years.

Though no particular communication had passed between Sascha, the baby's mother, and me, I became intensely curious about the baby. I knitted him a fine-gauge emerald green sweater with old-fashioned glass buttons in pale blue painted with cherries. I asked to be informed when she went into labor.

I believe now that I somehow bonded with my godson when he was in the womb. I was fresh from surgery and a life-threatening illness, so some psychic channels may have been more alive in me, or the baby himself may have been calling me, if you believe in that sort of thing.

Malidoma Some, in his book *Of Water and the Spirit*, talks about what happens when a baby is expected among his tribe, the Dagara, in its villages in Africa to determine "the life mission of the incoming soul." He writes: "A few months before birth, when the grandchild is still a fetus, a ritual called a 'hearing' is held.... During the ritual, the incoming soul takes the voice of the mother...and answers every question the priest asks.

"The living must know who is being reborn, where the soul is from, why it chose to come here, and what gender it has chosen.... Some souls ask that specific things be made ready for their arrival—talismanic power objects, medicine bags, metal objects.... They do not want to forget who they are and what they have come here to do."

———————

After Ishi was born, I went over to Sascha and Rune's to deliver the sweater. Sascha lay in semidarkness, nursing the tiny creature. I left my offering of the sweater and went away.

Ishi was a towheaded boy with large blueberry-colored eyes and a well-developed sense of humor. I fell in love with him and spent a lot of time with him in the early part of his life. The gift he gave me was one of heart; the love I felt for him was joyful and uncomplicated.

As a toddler, Ishi became obsessed with tools and liked to swagger around under the weight of the tool belt his father, Rune, had made him, constantly making repairs to the house, connecting his orange extension cords, imitating his dad as he practiced carpentry and drumming.

As he grew into a child, we played together and laughed. My best friend, Lou, once asked him, "Ishi, what do you do with Sue?"

"We walk around together and say funny things and make each other laugh," he said.

"That's funny," Lou said. "That's what she and I do too."

During Ishi's first few years, Sascha and Rune lived in a big house on College Avenue in the Elmwood district of Berkeley. I would go over there for a few hours before my job as a night copy editor and take Ishi for a walk in his stroller or play with him in the backyard. Often on Saturdays I took him to lunch at a neighborhood Chinese restaurant called King Yen.

It would never have occurred to me that taking a two- or three-year-old to lunch could be so pleasurable and entertaining, but it was. Sometimes it was like being with a child, and sometimes like being with a very old grownup in a child's body. One day, as we were eating lunch, Ishi put his face very close to mine, looked me straight in the eyes, and asked, "Who *are* you?" It was a profound question. I believe the source of our connection puzzled us both.

I've always liked children of three or four and was close to all my nieces and nephews at this age, but this was different. Ishi and I had a bond that seemed to have been forged in some ancient place, another life, on a soul plane neither one of us could touch.

I was at the right age too to play a grandmotherly role in his life. I had the patience to sit with him at the hardware store as he arranged tools in the various toolboxes or to accompany him on his rounds in the neighborhood. I also noticed that I was not the only person he drew into his sphere. Throughout his babyhood several other grownups participated in his life. They included one who years later became Sascha's husband after she and Rune had broken up.

One particular day from this time stands out for me. Ishi and I had gone for a walk in the neighborhood and stopped to buy lollipops at the grocery store. We both liked those Tootsie Roll pops that are red on the outside and chocolate when you reach the core. We sat on a bench in front of the Buttercup Bakery to savor our lollipops. He leaned against me and we swung our legs back and forth below the bench. For me, it was a perfect moment of happiness.

Grandparents often describe the sort of besotted love for their grandchildren that astounds them with its intensity and delight. I suppose Ishi and I had the proper age difference; at times our relationship was like that of grandparent and grandchild, but at other times it was pure friendship, such as one would have with a peer.

At times we were coconspirators, plotting mischief. Other times we were comedians or confidants. Sometimes, when he was fragile or under the weather, he sat next to me and held my ball of yarn as I knitted, unrolling it to release the thread as it became needed. This seemed to calm him, and the thread assumed almost a primal symbolism as umbilicus and connector.

It reminded me of another time, when my daughter had had surgery. I went to Napa, where she lived, to take care of her. We sat outside in the sunshine on the farm where she was staying, and she held my ball of yarn as I knitted.

This memory surfaces often for me, especially now that my daughter has taken up knitting. I sit with her in that same spot under the trees in Napa, helping her with her projects. Though a beginner, she has so much natural ability that I sometimes wonder if she absorbed the knitting I did while pregnant with her, osmotically through the womb.

————

I can remember times when my daughter was a newborn baby when I became lost in the pure milky bliss of new motherhood. I recall my first glimpse into her eyes as engendering a love so profound and overpowering it dwarfed anything I had ever experienced.

The love I felt for my godchild was different. Not so powerful, more peaceful and easy. I did feel my relationship with him entailed a responsibility, to be sure. There was no way I was going to waltz into his life for a minute and then disappear. I still have a friendship with him, although now, at ten, he sometimes seems to be in the first throes of adolescence, more interested in his peers. He remains, as he was in early childhood, extremely intelligent, always busy with Legos, building with wood, or now, preoccupied with computers and basketball, with a fine sense of humor and fun.

Over the years I've knitted three sweaters for Ishi, the last two at his request. The second one was a mint green cotton pullover, with a Henley opening for buttons. I let him design it himself. The color, his favorite at the time, was his choice, and the placket, "with three buttons, no collar," as he dictated, also was his idea.

I measured Ishi and made the sweater to his specifications but decorated it with three rainbow buttons. The rainbows were encased in clear plastic. When I gave Ishi the sweater, we were at a public place. He sat on the steps for a long time contemplating the buttons, wondering how the rainbows had gotten trapped inside the plastic.

Most recently he asked me to knit him a sweater for snowboarding. In my life it is only Ishi or Shuna whom I allow the privilege of dictating what to knit, though I have knitted some small things for friends, hats or scarves, at their requests when I could.

Like Shuna and me, Ishi is picky and opinionated. He wanted solid blue. He already has his guy preferences, no pockets, buttons, or anything fancy, just plain blue. I went to the yarn store and found a cashmere and wool blend in a nice shade of navy. It was called baby cashmerino. When I showed the yarn to Ishi, he took it out of the bag, held it to his face, and snuggled into it, enjoying its softness and warmth. That was my answer to whether or not he would like it.

I really can't say why this child remains so close inside my heart and why I so much treasure having him as a presence in my life. Everyone who sees us together notices the great love that passes between us. Both of us can't help lighting up when we see each other. Yet we are unrelated by blood or anything either of us can understand.

I know the time is coming when I shall have to let him go. The more he becomes concerned with "being cool," more like other kids he knows, the rarer become the times when he flings himself into my arms and invites me on an adventure. But that too is OK. It was never my job to bring him up, just to be there when he needed me, another grownup in his life to give him unconditional love.

Knitting for love should have its own separate category. First there is knitting for the sake of knitting, for the love of knitting itself. Then there is knitting to express your love for a person in a unique way. Perhaps those two should be reversed; I don't know. But love is a definite part of knitting, perhaps the reason so many of us like to knit for babies, even those who aren't our own.

One Christmas recently I made Shuna a sweater she wanted. My daughter is androgynous and dresses like a boy. She is also slender and has difficulty finding clothes to fit. I took her measurements and noted her preferences. She wanted a V-neck pullover vest, "like the ones Catholic schoolboys wear in pictures, tight, to fit over a shirt and tie."

Though in retrospect the sweater would probably have been better constructed of wool, I ordered some rich brown cashmere by mail order from Patternworks and found an old Penny Straker pattern for a tight vest with cables. Normally I like to feel and smell any yarn I use, consider it in my hands before making an investment. But the advent of mail-order Internet sources for yarn has been so helpful, and I have had such good luck with it, that I went ahead and bought the yarn.

It was soft and wonderful to work, with a pronounced halo and deep color, but it stretched out a bit more than I would have liked. This is sometimes a disadvantage of working with yarn that is too soft, if there is such a thing. Still, the sweater I made my daughter fitted her perfectly, length and width to her own dimensions, style to her preference. She wears it over a shirt and tie and likes to be photographed in this particular outfit.

It was gratifying for me with both these children that I had come so far in my knitting that I could make them what they wanted, exactly to fit. I enjoyed seeing them in the sweaters I had made, material proofs of my feelings for them, unique items that couldn't be purchased in stores.

Most of all, what I valued in these sweaters was the love that had gone into them, strong affections very close in feeling to prayer. Whether they are prayers for protection, prayers for welcoming, or prayers for letting go, the power of prayer figures in our knitting as we knit for people we love.

I have come to believe that love is ultimately mysterious, a gift from the Creator, a gift of grace. Our happiness comes from loving and being loved, and the work we do with our hands is tied in with it. "Hands to work, hearts to God," the Shakers used to say. Can it be that we become more capable of loving when our hands engage in creation and that those around us who are hurting or vulnerable are soothed and succored by being tied to the movements of our hands?

It has been one of the great joys of my life to have given birth to and brought up a daughter, who has been my life's companion, and another unexpected sort of joy that in my middle years I was given the gift of a godson, a golden child who opened my heart to easy, uncomplicated love.

4. Last of the Marlboro Men

SOME MEN SHOULD COME WITH A WARNING.

Billy (as I'll call him) approached me in a way no man ever had. He asked me about my knitting.

I was at a twelve-step event with my friend Lou. Both of us had been in recovery from addiction for many years. We were in the courtyard of Laney College, a junior college in Oakland. I was sitting on a bench knitting. I had noticed two men close by talking to each other and occasionally glancing my way, but I didn't think anything of it until one of them came over to me.

"I know how to do that," he said to me. "I know how to knit and purl. My grandmother taught me when I was a kid so I wouldn't bite my nails."

If it was a pickup line, it was one I had never

heard before. Few men approach a woman who is knitting, fewer still to talk about it.

"Oh, really?" I said. I was thinking, "Well. A man who can knit." I quickly went to a favorite fantasy: having a sleeve slave, someone to knit sleeves or the more tedious parts of any project. I had recently seen pictures of husbands and wives in the British Isles knitting Guernsey sweaters together, working on different parts of the piece.

The guy was kind of sparkly and appealing. He was tall and thin, with salt-and-pepper hair, a graying mustache, and China blue eyes. He was so charismatic I did not at first realize he was missing many of his teeth.

Later in our relationship, I read a description of the character John Laroche in Susan Orlean's book *The Orchid Thief* that reminded me of my first meeting with Billy. Laroche, Orlean writes, was "sharply handsome, in spite of the fact that he is missing all his front teeth." She also describes him as having "the posture of al dente spaghetti," a typical Billy slouch.

Billy had crinkly lines around his eyes, all the marks of a hard life. Like me, he was a recovering drug addict. Unlike me, he was just getting started with his recovery. When we met, I had twelve years clean. He had about six months.

There was also humor and spirit in his face. And charm. Oh, God. I've always been a sucker for charm. And failed to spot it when it came my way. He had a deep, sonorous voice. We chatted for a while, and I found myself so magnetically drawn to him that it was all I could do not to follow him around.

I didn't plan to fall in love. I thought that part of my life was over. I was middle-aged and solitary, mostly content with being alone.

Famous last words. Or as the torch song goes, "Comes love, nothing can be done."

────────

Billy's arrival in my life, in the fall of 1998, coincided with the first of a series of lace projects I undertook following the pattern for the Kerry Blue Shawl, named for its color, a gray-blue wool, and probably its county of origin in Ireland.

The great thing about the Kerry Blue is that it is a sampler of various lace patterns, which staves off boredom for the knitter and produces a complex and beautiful finished effect. It is so satisfying to knit that I ended up making several versions of the shawl, each corresponding to a phase of my relationship with Billy.

I could not obtain yarn in the gray-blue of the original, but I purchased a cone of slightly brighter blue laceweight wool from a mill in New England by mail order, and off I went on the great lace journey.

The shawl is supposed to begin at the center with twelve stitches on double-pointed needles. It is divided into four triangular pieces and grows by means of yarnover increases on either side of four two-stitch ribs. From its twelve-stitch beginning, it eventually expands to over a thousand stitches at its outer perimeter, not counting the border.

I tried to master lace knitting at the same time I was trying to understand love. I believe that whatever you experience is recorded in your handwork. So my awkwardness, the reawakening of my sensuality, the confusion, elation, insecurity, and pain all somehow got recorded in that first blue shawl.

As the great jazzman Charlie Parker said, "If you don't live it, it won't come out your horn."

I began the shawl on an evening shortly after I had begun seeing Billy. I sat on my couch trying to arrange the twelve stitches on the four needles. I don't like double-pointed needles. Though I have been knitting for more than forty years, I have never made a pair of socks and will do almost anything to avoid double-pointed needles.

After hours of awkwardness, frustration, and failure, I put the twelve stitches on a small circular needle and decided I would graft the seam when the circle became large enough to close.

I improvised, as I was to try to improvise my relationship with Billy. It probably worked out better in the shawl. I ended up giving the shawl to a woman I've loved all my life, but my feeling for her was a different sort of love, more companionate, packed with the formidable power of longtime female friendship. The shawl now lives with her in Amsterdam. I hope it warms her and reminds her of my love.

————

Intimacy is a difficult area for me. Over the years of my recovery I became aware that intimacy was my last frontier. I could maintain lifelong friendships with women, but I couldn't seem to succeed in an intimate partnership with a person of the opposite sex.

Lou, who grew up like my mother with a passel of brothers, said it was because I didn't understand men. Something was missing in my ability to grasp the thinking and behavior patterns of the male animal. I set out to repair this deficit, invisibly weaving, as it were, over the holes. But I can't say it ever really worked, though it did produce an awful lot of knitting.

I had begun at the beginning, trying to redeem my relationship with my father, my first and primary male figure. All my problems in relationships could be traced back to Dad. I grew up believing he did not love me, the result of an awkward start when he returned from World War II. A toddler mystified by this new person in my life, I failed to greet him with the proper affection. Our estrangement for the whole of my childhood and early adulthood colored every interaction I ever had with a man.

By the time I met Billy, my father and I were involved in an effort to reestablish our bond. I had also begun forging a relationship with a little boy, my godson, Ishi. I went into my affair with Billy in that same openhearted spirit.

When you're clean and sober, it's difficult to fall into bed with someone and pretend you don't know what you're doing. Every step is conscious and not always comfortable. Both the pleasures and the pains are experienced without the buffer of mood-altering substances. And the vulnerability can be excruciating.

Some months after I first met Billy, we went out for coffee in

Alameda after a meeting. In that short time I learned everything I would need to know about him. I knew that he was a liar and a womanizer and would probably use drugs again.

I chose to ignore all that information and dived headfirst into the icy rushing stream.

———————

We definitely had chemistry between us. I hadn't been in love in quite a while. I used to watch lovers in public places with a mixture of puzzlement and incomprehension. What made them intertwine like that? I wondered. How do you get that sort of thing started?

The truth was I was touch-deprived. The first time Billy touched me, I was a goner. We lay on the couch in my house, and he pulled me over him, curling me on his chest like a small child. Then he stroked the top of my head the way my mother used to put me to sleep when I was a baby. His hands were large and gentle, and I warmed to his touch like a starving man to a bowl of soup.

My attraction to Billy was so intense that whenever I saw him, parts of my body would find themselves in proximity to his. Our legs would become entwined, or our feet would touch; our shoulders and upper arms would come together into one unit, or our hands would clasp or our lips conjoin or all the rest.

He was fun in bed too, in a way I knew was the sign of a born womanizer, but I swept that insight under the carpet. Also, something happened to me with him that I had never experienced before.

When we lay in bed together face-to-face, the bones at the center of my chest seemed to open, and my heart yearned toward his in a way that was physically palpable. We could lie together and exchange energy heart to heart in almost a figure eight pattern. I took that sign of my heart opening as a good thing, although it made me terribly vulnerable. It didn't last long. The first time Billy broke my heart, those bones in my chest closed shut and would not open again, though we spent several years after that going back and forth in the come here, go away dance of attraction.

With Billy, my shell cracked open. Like it or not, my heart came out of hiding.

Once, in a not entirely complimentary spirit, Billy called me Velcro girl. I had to point out to him that in order for Velcro to work, it required two pieces to stick to each other. Depending on his mood, he liked to pretend that he wasn't really involved in our love affair. He broke up with me regularly and came back just as often. Painful splits and dramatic reconciliations were his stock-in-trade.

The insecurity and uncertainty this produced in me drove me to search for explanations or predictions about our future in every astrology and self-help book I could find at the Barnes and Noble near my job. I was a mass of quivering nerves, constantly wondering: Why did he leave? When will he come back? Can it possibly all work out in the end?

In Chinese astrology he was a dragon and I was a sheep. Dragons are charismatic and changeable. Breakups and reunions are part of their pattern, as is their irresistibility to the opposite sex. Sheep, on the other hand, crave security and creativity.

"You know what happens when dragons meet sheep?" Billy once asked me.

"No," I said. "What?"

"Chomp, chomp," he said.

———

In February 1999, shortly after my love affair with Billy had begun and just after we had spent our first night together, I went to Key West to celebrate my father's eightieth birthday. Sheila and Jon, my sister and brother-in-law, had restored a blue and white wooden house. To get there, I flew across the country on a jet, then to Key West on a puddle jumper so small that the pilot opened the windows to get some air.

I was in the first flush of love and more than a little obsessed and unsure. Every time I called Billy on the phone, I didn't know what I would find. I tried to fortify myself with rounds of tai chi or long walks around the town, and the physical activity helped, but there was really no cure for the jitters that plagued me.

It had been a long time since I had fallen in love. I was astonished to find that adolescent feelings of giddy infatuation and plummeting despair could still surface in my being as though I were a gawky fourteen-year-old experiencing my first real crush.

In Key West I paced like a caged cat, played music to distract myself, vacillated between elation and depression like some sappy love song from the 1930s.

My father took my nephew Darryl and me down to Mallory Square to look at the sunsets. Mallory Square is where everyone in Key West gathers at sunset, a tourist attraction and mecca for street performers. It feels like the edge of the world. With its trade wind breezes and rustling palms, Key West has the heated atmosphere of an old colonial town in the Caribbean, sort of how I imagine New Orleans, steamy scandals hidden behind hedges of honeysuckle and bougainvillea. The town was beautiful; the sunsets were spectacular. I thought of Billy.

My father enjoyed himself. He liked to explore new places. I worked on my blue shawl. It was the most demanding lace I had ever attempted. But each new pattern had a rhythmic complexity that carried me along. With each repetition of pattern, the shawl grew and became strikingly blue. I made up a little ditty to go with my work and my state of mind: "The house was blue, his eyes were blue, the shawl was blue, and I was too." When Billy was indifferent to me on the phone or evasive or could not be found, I listened to a Keb' Mo' song that advised me to remember that if nobody loved me and I felt neglected and alone, I could always love myself.

I must have driven my parents to distraction with the music I played, a reprise of my teenage years. When I spoke on the phone to Billy, he hinted that he had gotten involved with someone else. He thought we had broken up, he didn't want to be serious, whatever evasion he could come up with at the moment. I went from wild hopefulness to deep despondency in the blink of an eye. I think my parents and my sister were surprised and a little disturbed to see me in this state of massive confusion; I had been stable and solitary for so many years.

Still, we had a good time. My father's health was in decline but not yet to the point where he couldn't travel. My mother watched over him, fussing about his meals and his pills. She didn't like to leave the comfort and predictability of her own home. My father's eightieth was a momentous occasion. None of my grandparents or any relatives my parents could remember had made it to eighty, and my father had been living on borrowed time for a good ten years.

Sometimes when you look back on events in memory, you find more going on than you thought at the time. It's like viewing an old photograph with a magnifying glass and suddenly realizing the significance of something in the background that seemed unimportant then. In retrospect now, I recall my father's happiness more clearly than I remember my nervous preoccupation with my love affair. In time and memory, background and foreground have traded places. I recall the Keb' Mo' music and the magenta vanda orchid my sister received as a housewarming gift more clearly than I remember what Billy told me on the phone.

———

When I arrived home from that trip to Florida, the phone was ringing as I walked in the door. Billy was on the other end. He came over and didn't leave for a couple of months.

Then we revived the break up, make up routine he once called "bungee love." Or in a fancier version, "bungee love with freight train."

When Billy and I were first dating, I worked at Jack London Square. He had a job nearby. He would call me when he got off work late in the afternoon, at about the same time there was a natural lull in my editing schedule. I would go out to meet him for coffee. We hung around the plaza in the square, drinking coffee, holding hands, having a romance on the waterfront along the Oakland estuary, surrounded by seagulls, container ships, loading cranes, sunshine, rainstorms, and sky.

A freight train runs past Jack London Square. At certain times of day it has a very long procession of containers that stops dead for several minutes at a time on its journey. Its passage can seem interminable.

One day I was on the terrace at Starbucks, waiting for Billy to come. A freight train was stopped in front of the square. All of a sudden I saw Billy climb up one of the couplings between the cars and drop down gracefully on his long, rangy legs. Then he looked up at me and smiled broadly.

"I was watching you do that," I said when he appeared on the terrace.

"I was hoping you would," he said.

Those were heady times in our relationship. One day in a drenching rainstorm Billy covered me with his coat to walk me back to my job, getting soaked himself in the process. I am not the sort of woman people hasten to protect, and I enjoyed the feeling of being cherished and cared for.

Another cold afternoon we sat at a table outside Jack's Bistro, drinking coffee. Billy had been driving a truck all day. He took hold of my hand across the table. "This morning," he said, "that song 'When a Man Loves a Woman' came on the radio. I couldn't help thinking of you."

That night, inexplicably, he stood me up. I kept looking out the window for his car, keeping myself busy by learning a new song on the guitar. The song was "Oh, the Wind and Rain," which Jerry Garcia sang in his quavery tenor apart from the Grateful Dead. It's an old ballad about a girl whose sister pushes her into the river out of jealousy. A passing musician comes and fishes the girl out of the water. He makes a fiddle from the drowned girl's breastbone, using her delicate fingerbones for pegs and her long yellow hair to string the bow. "And the only tune that fiddle would play was 'Oh, the dreadful wind and rain.'"

The song was heartrending, like the experience of being stood up by your great new love. Of course I should have quit him right then and there. But I didn't. I couldn't. I was too hooked in. Hooked like a trout, as one of my friends once said about his dope habit.

That was the first of many mysteries, comings and goings, unpredictable hesitancies, and equally unexpected returns. In the good moments of our relationship I read *Men Are from Mars, Women Are from Venus* and justified Billy's behavior by imagining he had withdrawn to his cave on Mars to build rocket ships to get back to Venus, or whatever it is John Gray says men do.

In the bad moments I read *Addiction to Love* by Susan Peabody and compared Billy with the author's description of "the seductive withholder," an immature narcissist incapable of empathy with the feelings of others.

No matter what I read, I was baffled and off-balance, ecstatic or sobbing, reduced to a state of confusion and upset. Yet I steadily worked on the blue shawl, completing first one motif, then another. I found I loved this particular form of knitting. In making lace, the knitter captures emptiness, enclosing holes formed by the yarnovers with the solid bits of knitting. The contrasting open and closed stitches form the pictorial quality of the lace.

I made the border in an ancient pattern called Ocean Waves. Each sawtooth repetition has an internal swirl like the curling of a wave and ends in a point at its edges. All the patterns in the shawl originate in the Shetland Islands, where knitted shawls were famed for being so fine they could be drawn through wedding rings. One of the patterns was the feather and fan, which I used for the qiviut shawl and which became a lifelong favorite for me. I sometimes teach feather and fan in beginning lace knitting classes, and I have knitted it countless times in delicate scarves that employ the unpredictable effects of hand-painted yarn to play against the waving scallops of the lace.

The knitting was finished at a time when we were back together. Billy, who had once made a living knotting hammocks with an ancient hand-weaving technique, loved the shawl. "Someone has to know how great you are," he said as he watched me block the shawl on my living room floor.

I tried to take lessons from knitting into our relationship with sometimes comical effect. One thing that is important in lace, and indeed all knitting, is to hold the yarn with the proper tension, loosely enough to obtain fluidity in the stitches but tightly enough to avoid gapping.

"I'm trying not to hold on too tightly," I told Billy one night. "I'm trying to hold on just loosely enough to maintain contact while letting you spin out as much as you need."

"The trouble is that I'm not yarn," he answered in an acerbic tone.

Over the course of my affair with Billy I made several versions of the Kerry Blue Shawl. In later years it occurred to me that the secret weapon that had enabled me to endure all those mood swings and crazy times was the cultivation of emptiness I practiced while knitting the shawls: blue, white, and finally black.

In the design of this shawl, because of the four ribs that connect the triangles, emptiness expands the piece. I found this a fitting and consoling spiritual metaphor that helped ease the pain of emotional ups and downs. Spacious emptiness was a state of mind I aspired to, and here it was taking place under the patient workings of my hands.

In times of emotional difficulty, I sometimes tried to insert emptiness into the day's events in much the same way I used yarnovers for lace in the shawls. Some nights I was in so much pain over our love affair that sleep eluded me. In the middle of the night I would creep out to the living room, wrap myself in the darkness and warmth of a large woven black cashmere shawl, and sink deeply into meditation until I gained a larger perspective, the perspective of eternity. I expanded those moments with emptiness to create distance from the pain, to become both immersed in and separated from the present moment, to remind myself that I belonged to another reality, a larger consciousness, a vast and fruitful emptiness of luminous blackness and primal light.

Just as I enjoyed stark emptiness in the spacious landscapes of the Great Plains or the Florida Everglades, the deep quiet, the long view to the horizon, I liked my mind, as much as humanly possible, to be empty of chatter, free of attachments, detached from pain.

When I was practicing tai chi chuan, something that didn't happen often because I was the flakiest of practitioners, I repeated the slow rounds of movements until I felt a slight internal expansion. This was a subtle sensation, something like a quickening, the first feeling of a baby turning inside your pregnant belly, or the realization that your lungs have suddenly expanded to accommodate more air. When my father was dying and I went to his bedside in the middle of the night to sit and meditate, the only indication I had that I had made contact with his spirit was a slight internal lifting. Still, the inner world is a place of infinite vastness and precious consolation, and I counted myself fortunate to know how to get there.

By day I knitted the lacy blue shawl. Within it was contained the beginnings of my relationship with Billy, the spacious sunsets of Key West, companionable times with my father and family, happiness, heartbreak, and ordinary life. At night I meditated. Within my meditation was contained the eternal life of the spirit, a pure, unchanging, and incorruptible consciousness, the knowledge of my inner being, a larger view of the soul's pure purpose and a distance from the petty concerns of everyday life.

Both sprang from the same source, the deep well of emptiness that paradoxically contains everything that is or ever could be. This emptiness soothes, instructs, expands. It grew my knitting and gave me solace. It reminded me of a folksong I'd always liked:

Trouble in mind, trouble in mind
Trouble in mind, trouble in mind
Trouble in mind, trouble in mind
God's gonna ease my trouble in mind.

5. Every Good-bye Ain't Gone

FROM BILLY I LEARNED THE TRUTH OF THE AFRICAN-American folk expression "Every shut eye ain't 'sleep, every good-bye ain't gone." But it took me a while to learn it.

When I got together with Billy, my godson, Ishi, was about four. His father, Rune, used to bring him to a twelve-step meeting we both attended on Sunday mornings, and I would take Ishi for a walk or entertain him outside while Rune attended the meeting.

One sunny Sunday morning I was outside the meeting with Ishi when Billy, carrying a cup of coffee, came loping down the street.

"Can I talk to you?" he asked when he got close to me.

"Uh, yeah."

"I don't want to do this anymore," he said. "It's over between us. I mean it this time."

As he said it, he was sitting next to me, so close he was practically in my lap, with his hand on my leg and kissing my cheek. Talk about your mixed messages.

I burst into tears.

"I'm sorry," he said. "I just keep coming back to that. I have to let you go."

Ishi was walking back and forth on the sidewalk in front of us, peering into my face to see what was going on.

"My relationship with Ishi opened my heart," I told Billy. "I used to think that was a good thing...until now."

Rune came out of the meeting and sat with me. We watched Billy walk back up the block. "He's a sexy guy," said Rune. "There's something about him, the way he swings his arms."

"I know," I said miserably. "I wish I weren't so hung up on him, but I am."

We went to lunch at Picante, a Mexican restaurant in Berkeley. Ishi stayed close to me.

"What did you think of that guy," I asked him, "the one I was talking to outside the meeting?"

"He's a bad man, Sue," said Ishi.

"Why?"

"Because he was hugging and kissing you. And nobody hugs and kisses you but me."

One evening about a year into our relationship, Billy and I sat talking on the stairs of the communal house where he lived. It was late July, my favorite time of year. The yellow Rainier cherries were in season; jacaranda trees were dropping fat purple blossoms all over everything; it was almost time to go to the river. But I couldn't enjoy it because Billy had broken up with me again and I was bereft.

In those days I believed I could talk him into being with me, reason with him, convince him it was better for us to stay together.

I wore a red and white polka-dotted dress I hoped would charm him. The huge umbrella palm that had been growing for a hundred years in front of the house arched its fronds over us, and the neglected rosebush at the foot of the stairs rained small red petals on the ground.

It was a perfect night for romance, but there was none to be had.

"But why?" I said. "Why don't you want to be with me?"

I hate to admit I was practically begging, but what did I know about love? It had never occurred to me that love was something granted to you as a gift of grace, settled over you like a soft blanket, that you didn't need to do or say anything to earn it.

"I don't want this relationship," Billy said. "Why can't you just accept it? You were fine by yourself before you met me."

"The trouble is," I said, "I can't go back to the person I was before you touched me."

I didn't know that it wasn't my fault, that Billy came and went according to the mysterious dictates of his own emotional landscape, and that he would return of his own accord soon after I returned from my trip to the Russian River. Which made it a waste of a perfectly good vacation that I spent pining for lost love.

———

No matter how badly you think you're doing, something that belies your private grief is always happening in the exterior. That summer the osprey, which we had been observing for years as it flew by, whistling, twice a day in search of its dinner, acquired a whole new family we had never seen before. Theresa brought another friend to the river; Lou's son Nick turned into a teenager.

Billy or no Billy, life went on. The cranky middle-aged ladies played Lucille for hours in the evening; the green water meandered around the bend; the redwoods gave off their clean aroma and majestic presence; I practiced tai chi on the rise above the river until I felt that small internal expansion.

From Tina's extensive CD collection, I selected a compilation of Taj Mahal's music. I listened to songs he had recorded with the Pointer Sisters. Especially "The Little Red Hen Blues," in which someone asks the little red hen whatever happened to that little red rooster she was seeing. "The rooster don't come around as much as he used to," the questioner notes. And the little red hen answers, "You know he's long gone, like a turkey through the co-o-orn."

Theresa had to interpret the last line for me. And the Lucille players pretended I wasn't driving them crazy with my sadness over Billy and his most recent abandonment.

Soon enough he came back again.

———

That time he stayed for quite a while. For a time we enjoyed a period of relative stability and happiness. Every night after work Billy tapped on my window and spent the night. His truck was parked in front of my house. He told me he loved me. Mutual friends began to think of us as a twosome. I felt as though Billy had made a commitment to our relationship and was determined to see it through. Though we didn't always get along together, the comings and goings were less dramatic, the ground beneath our feet was more firm.

"Whatever you do," the ladies at the Knitting Basket, my local yarn store, said, "don't knit him a sweater. That will jinx the relationship for sure." Linda, who owned the store, and Betty, who worked there, had by then seen me through the whole affair. The Knitting Basket was the first place I went for comfort and consolation whenever anything troubled me.

I didn't knit Billy a sweater, but I did begin another version of the Kerry Blue Shawl. This one was white, milk white lace, and comparisons to wedding attire were all but inevitable.

The white shawl was for Georgette, the wife of my Rolfer, Michael Salveson, but I held the thought of marriage in my mind as I worked. Somewhat unbelievably, considering our past, the idea of marriage had arisen in our relationship. We had talked about it, joked about it, and, ever the romantic dreamer, I fantasized a hippie wedding on top of Mount Tamalpais, the kind we used to have in the old days of the sixties. "But the ceremony of the bells and lace still veils this restless fool here," Joni Mitchell wrote in "Song for Sharon," one of her many songs about "love's illusions."

It was not the only fantasy I held of Billy. He was a construction guy, in the building trades. Like my father, he could fix cars and all things mechanical, and he understood the inner workings of electricity, plumbing, and home repair. I thought perhaps we would buy a house together and fix it up. On some level I believe I thought Billy was my last great hope for love and togetherness. I used to feel unmoored when he left me, bereft and adrift, though I realized the foolishness of counting on someone so unstable to tether me to dry land.

No one ever accused me of being a realist.

The yarn for the white shawl was a laceweight wool from Straw into Gold, a huge knitting and weaving store in Berkeley that has since gone out of business. I started out with two skeins; each skein had about twelve hundred yards, and the yarn was exceedingly fine. By contrast, a more typical ball of yarn has about a hundred or so yards to it.

One night Billy and I had some sort of disagreement. He slept, but I couldn't. I decided to go into the kitchen and wind the white lace yarn into a ball. About a third of the way through, I hit a snag, and the yarn became tangled. I tried in vain to untangle it as more and more strands became hopelessly knotted into a solid mess. My frustration boiled over, and I fell to the floor in tears, sobbing in the midst of the ruined white yarn and whatever wedding fantasies it had unleashed in me.

That should have been a sign to me, but never mind, I ignored it. Of all the versions of that lace shawl I ever knitted, the white was my favorite. As it grew, it seemed to absorb air and light and loft, frothing up like a confectionary creation. In the end it looked almost like a wedding cake. When I gave it to Michael, he was moved by its beauty.

"The pleasure was mine," I said. "It was like knitting a cloud."

Michael had ordered some ancient granite paving stones from China for the courtyard of his house. The stones would otherwise have been flooded by the damming of the Yangtze River. When they arrived from China, he placed each one by hand. The courtyard was beautiful, and the stones had the presence of ages.

"Didn't they hurt your back?" I asked.

"Let's put it this way," Michael said. "It was definitely not like knitting a cloud."

———

In the white lace shawl, as in the blue one that had come before it, I knitted the border in a long strip and then sewed it onto the body. This was an improvised solution but hardly ideal. When I blocked the white shawl on my mattress, parts of the border seaming tore and had to be repaired.

For several years I led a workshop called a Spiritual Knitting Retreat at the Esalen Institute in Big Sur, on the wild central coast of California. One year an accomplished lace knitter taught me how to knit the sawtooth border onto the shawl. This eliminated the need for binding off, which was no easy task with over a thousand stitches, and it also integrated the border more fully with the body of the shawl.

I used this technique to good effect in the last Kerry Blue Shawl I made in this series, the one that was black for mourning.

———————

There was one lesson from knitting that I could apply to my relationship with Billy, and I had many occasions to repeat it to myself. "The pattern doesn't lie," I would say about his comings and goings, his meanness, ambivalence, and various untruths. Whenever we got too close, he always cut and ran away. So I never felt too secure around him. When things were going well, I held my breath for the inevitable crash.

He did too. Once, in the midst of a particularly happy reconciliation, he said, "I wish it could always be like this."

"Why can't it?" I asked.

"Because it's us," he said.

The truth was that in matters of love I had my own pattern too. There was a certain type of man who always engaged me, drawing me into the cycle of unrequited love. Usually it was a handsome stranger, a cowboy loner, a seemingly shy and unassuming sort of guy who had managed to slide through life on his good looks and by charming women. Billy to a tee. I could superimpose his face and body on the likenesses of several men with whom I'd performed this dance, sometimes finding one indistinguishable from another.

But Billy had stolen my heart and in his own way loved me back. Though I'd done spiritual work for years to soften and open the heart, and though I'd experienced the expansion of feeling with Ishi, I had never before felt the physical sensation of an opening in the chest that I had with Billy.

That made it far more painful when he left.

———

There were so many comings and goings in the course of my relationship with Billy that I could hardly keep track of them all. The one that really rankled, the one I still can't quite forgive him for, was his leaving me for another woman when my father first fell gravely ill.

We had been together fairly steadily for at least a matter of months when he announced he had accepted a large job out of town. He would have to move to Santa Cruz for the duration of the job, he said, and would try to see me on weekends, but we would be spending far less time with each other.

He had been working as a handyman for a while, and I have to admit I never trusted him around the women whose homes he repaired. As it happened, I had good reason for my suspicions.

One Friday at work I got a phone call from my sister saying my father had been taken to intensive care in a hospital in Florida with a potentially fatal heart arrhythmia. I made immediate plans to go there.

When I was at home, Billy called and said he was back from Santa Cruz. "I'm so glad you're home," I said. "My father's in the hospital, and I have to go to Florida."

"I'll take a nap and come over later," he said.

He never came over, and he never called. The therapist I saw during the early days of my relationship with Billy said I should have gotten rid of him the first time he stood me up, instead of waiting around for a more devastating desertion. But as you can probably tell by now, I was no poster child for high self-esteem.

Still, I counted this one unforgivable. To me it was unconscionable that he would cause me this much extra worry when I was already frantic with anxiety.

Around this same time, a friend told me she had seen Billy's truck in Berkeley a lot during the time he was supposedly working in Santa Cruz. She thought he had taken up with the neighbor of a friend of hers; she had observed them flirting and holding hands.

When I confronted Billy, he said, "I love you, but I'm not in love with you." As though that made it all right. He admitted he was infatuated with Louise, the woman I had heard about, and had been looking for opportunities to break up with me.

I went off to Florida doubly distraught. My father was in bad shape in a hospital in Pompano Beach. I drove his van back and forth from my parents' home in Delray. Sometimes, driving alone at night, I howled with grief.

My father suffered cardiac arrest that time, a code blue, but the doctors pulled him out of it. The whole family showed up in Florida, and I believe it was the constant presence of his wife and four children, as well as the skill of the doctors, that got my father through that crisis.

By the time I arrived home, Billy was in a full-blown relationship with the other woman. I remember standing in the street outside his house in my prettiest summer dress, yellow with watercolored goldfish on it, wanting desperately for him to come back even as we argued about dividing our small stock of shared possessions.

We bickered back and forth. He said he preferred Louise to me because she was younger, thinner, blonder than I. He had no compunctions about using my insecurities to torment me. I later found out Louise had something else I didn't have, pills and plenty of them. She was chronically ill and in possession of permanent prescriptions for some highly addictive substances. Billy may have left me for another woman, but he was headed straight back into the arms of his true and original love, drugs.

Whatever the circumstances, it was over.

I began knitting a black shawl, black for grief. "He doesn't deserve your grief," said one of my knitting buddies, but that was beside the point. Feelings just are what they are. The yarn was the same as the white, but the black shawl was more technically accomplished than the previous two.

The inner landscape it represented was ravaged and barren.

During this time I clung to some lines from a Paul Simon song, "Graceland," that said "Losing love is like a window in your heart; Everybody sees you're blown apart."

I felt as though I had been cracked open, and there was a hole inside me where the wind blew through. Years later, after my friend Judith committed suicide, her husband, Ray, used the same language to describe his loss. "Wind still howls through the hole in my life," he wrote me in an e-mail.

During the course of my relationship with Billy, I had begun knitting and mastered the complexities of creating lace shawls. Now I was like a piece of lace myself, porous, full of holes.

———

It was surprisingly difficult to disengage from Billy. I needed him to fix my car. He had to do some repairs in my house. We relied on each other emotionally for a long time. His was the shoulder I cried on after my father died. I was the person he called when the events of September 11, 2001, began unfolding on TV. He was the first person I told about my shocking diagnosis of breast cancer at the end of 2002.

Though our relationship is long over, we still have an uncanny ability to communicate heart to heart. He was around here about six months ago, doing some carpentry work for a neighbor. He came by to hug me, and immediately that current of energy came alive and passed between our chests.

Over the years drugs have done strange things to Billy. He is not nearly so attractive as he once was. His skin is wrinkled beyond what it should be for his age. He seems to lack a force field around his body; he has no electrical sense of vitality emanating from his being, what some might call an aura. He's become emaciated and so gray that, as one friend of ours says, "He looks as though he's been dipped in flour."

Eventually I gave up hope of anything's ever getting better with Billy. He continues his downward spiral. Even with my own experience, I find it hard to believe he will get clean, and I know I can't be around a using addict. It may be healthy to have given up hope of fulfilling that particular dream, but it's also sad.

I sometimes think back on our relationship. I think of my erotic awakening after the desert of middle-aged solitude. At the time I met Billy, I'd been listening to Lucinda Williams's "Car Wheels on a Gravel Road." Williams's songs of love and sex had emboldened me to embark on a love affair after being alone for so long.

Unfortunately, it was a Randy Weeks song, recorded by Lucinda, that best described my relationship with Billy: "Well it's over, I know it, but I can't let go."

I think back over my whole romantic history, trying to untangle the threads, from childhood fantasies of cosmopolitan romance modeled on Fred Astaire and Ginger Rogers movies, with graceful dancing, witty repartee, elegant settings, and fabulous evening clothes, to teenage fantasies of Marlon Brando and James Dean, all jeans, black leather, and T-shirts with sleeves rolled up to hold packs of cigarettes. Tough on the outside, tender on the inside, revealing their inmost vulnerability to only one special girl.

Some of my college friends are still married to the men they wed out of college, now, more than thirty years later. I wonder why they stuck with it and I didn't. I wonder if I didn't purposely arrange things to wind up alone, from a love of solitude and fear of engulfment.

The whole area of love and relationship continues to mystify me. I sought intimacy with Billy. I knew it was a problem for me. I tend to be guarded and keep even people I love at a distance, yet I chose to let Billy in. It may have been a poor choice, but it was one I consciously made.

Whenever I went to therapists, usually in crazy times during relationships, they always said the same thing to me: "You can't love anyone else until you learn to love yourself."

Self-love. Healthy or narcissistic? Myth or reality? How did one get there? Usually I thought I'd been working on just that issue when the therapists brought me back to ground zero.

A friend recommended I read Pema Chodron, a student of Chogyam Trungpa, the late Tibetan rinpoche who established the Naropa Institute in Boulder, Colorado, and Gampo Abbey in Nova Scotia, where Pema is the director.

I began reading *When Things Fall Apart: Heart Advice for Diffi-*

cult Times. Suddenly the words became luminous. It is the nature of things to fall apart, Pema writes. No amount of controlling and worrying can keep them together; they fall apart and come together strictly of their own accord.

Impermanence is a permanent condition of our humanity. We can choose to embrace it and live with groundlessness, or we can frantically grasp for solid ground every time the bottom falls out.

Mainly what Pema advocates is a sort of self-acceptance. It is an acceptance of our full selves, with their divinity and universality, their characteristic flaws. We can find the beauty inside ourselves like a precious jewel shining through a heap of garbage.

I found her words strangely consoling. My life was what it was. I didn't lack romantic love and stability because there was something wrong with me. I hadn't even made particularly unfortunate choices. "The heart wants what it wants," my friend Pam used to say when she saw me with Billy in one of his more impaired states.

I was on the right track during those awful nights of arguments with Billy when I meditated to put emptiness into our relationship, to gain a perspective of eternity. The opening of the heart is a good thing, whether it is by recognition of our own mortality, the cracking apart of the shell by violent breaking, or a conscious expansion of compassion and loving-kindness, as much toward ourselves as toward others.

I try at times to practice Pema's brand of loving-kindness, to be a friend to myself. I attempt to see myself the way I wish others had seen me, through eyes of the heart. I try not to fall into romantic fantasy as anything but a reverie, a reflexive habit of mind, though it would be pleasant to feel again that stirring of physical attraction, that creature comfort of skin touching skin.

As for love and intimacy, I'll keep that as an open question. The end of the story hasn't been written yet. The fat lady still hasn't sung.

6. A House
Full of Sky

EVERY YEAR, WHEN WE COULD, MY FRIEND JUDYCAROL and I drove across South Dakota to Bear Butte, a volcanic laccolith that rises suddenly from the Great Plains near the Black Hills, a mountain sacred to the Sioux and Northern Cheyenne tribes.

Judycarol is like a sister to me. I met her around twenty years ago, when I landed up in a halfway house in St. Cloud, Minnesota. St. Cloud, a German Catholic town on the banks of the Mississippi River, northwest of the Twin Cities, was such foreign country to me that a counselor declared, "Here you're not a fish out of water, you're a fish in the desert." I was dazed and confused.

On my first day at the halfway house, another

resident, noting my disorientation, said, "Just wait until six o'clock. Judycarol will be here, and she'll run your life."

We struck up a friendship and have stayed in touch over the years, visiting back and forth. We also became what some people call road dogs, or traveling companions. It turned out we both have a love of western landscapes, Indian sites, and long trips across empty scenery by car.

I used to like to take needlepoint canvases along on these trips. One year I had a canvas painted with different-colored butterflies. It was the first time I had used number five perle cotton thread on eighteen-mesh canvas. In fineness, this is somewhere between petit point and the more typical needlepoint done with tapestry wool on fourteen-mesh canvas. The perle cotton gives the work a hard, pleasantly knobby surface with a slight sheen, almost as though it were beaded. I changed the background from yellow to sky blue and shaded the butterflies in yellows and oranges, rose, and pale green.

I felt very free as I worked on this canvas in the evenings in motels along our route, after Judycarol and I had spent the day driving. The needlepoint felt like a vacation to me, an activity with no deadline, no obligation, no complication, no shaping, just a simple pleasurable way to pass the time. As an added benefit, I can recreate the vacation in my mind now, years later, when I look at the needlepoint.

Judycarol and I took a lot of trips together. We went across northern Montana to Glacier National Park; we drove the north shore of Lake Superior, across the Trans-Canada Highway and down through Lake of the Woods in northern Minnesota. But our usual vacation spot was western South Dakota, near the Black Hills and one of our favorite places, Spearfish Canyon.

We crossed the Missouri River at Mobridge, South Dakota. The rolling hills on the far side of the river, the Missouri Breaks, seemed so familiar to me, so much a place I had known and loved forever, that I craved it sometimes with a tangible longing.

Over the years the landscape of the Great Plains began to affect me profoundly. The simple palette of spring green and pale blue, the song of the meadowlark, prairie falcons lighting on round bales of hay, distant yet visible lightning storms, my ability to see miles to the horizon: All became part of a terrain I loved. Sometimes when I am knitting at home and the movie *Dances with Wolves* comes on television, I watch it with the sound turned off just to see the South Dakota sky.

The San Francisco Bay Area, where I live, is no doubt beautiful, but if I am away from the plains too long, I begin to yearn for the vast sky, the open vistas, the unobstructed sight lines of the plains. The writer Louise Erdrich, who grew up in North Dakota, has called this longing "horizon sickness."

In the midst of my life in California, I often experience the pull of horizon sickness. I begin to crave what Ann Jauregui, a Berkeley therapist and the author of *Epiphanies*, identifies as a medicinal remedy in and of itself, the long view.

I believe I grew to love Florida, during bird-watching trips I took with my father to the Everglades, partly because the simple combination of grass and big sky, the sense of immense space, air, and distance, reminded me of the plains. The Everglades are called the River of Grass, as the plains can seem like an ocean of grass.

I believe these open landscapes, though seemingly desolate and lonely, can paradoxically release us from the burden of our own loneliness. My father loved the open landscapes of the West, as did his father before him. Perhaps I inherited the craving for space the way I inherited my skill with a needle and thread, in the blood and in the genes. Who knows?

———

From Mobridge, Judycarol and I drove east for a ways, through the Standing Rock reservation, where Sitting Bull is buried, then south down to Eagle Butte, the unofficial capital of the Cheyenne River Sioux Nation. Cheyenne River is the home of Green Grass, where the sacred pipe of the Lakota, said to be the original brought by White Buffalo Calf Woman, is held by Arvol Looking Glass.

Once we passed Faith (there is also a Reliance, South Dakota) we had a long drive to Sturgis and Bear Butte. They are mostly gone now, but at one time you couldn't drive more than ten or twenty miles across South Dakota without passing the ruins of long-abandoned homesteads. The sight of these houses is haunting; the hardscrabble lives and tragic histories they represent can all but break your heart.

The landscape is so stark and austere that any color stands

out. Once I saw a red boxcar sitting on a track with both doors flung open. You could see right through it to the grass and the sky. The red rectangle framing a square of spring green and robin's-egg blue sky was so striking an image that it made me wish I were a painter to capture the drama of those three simple colors.

One abandoned homestead we saw stood tall and intact except for its missing roof beams, which let in the sky. I thought of it as a house full of sky, and the image caught my imagination. The house was damaged yet made more beautiful by its ruin, in the same way that a broken heart can let in more light, embrace intimations of divinity, begin an understanding of compassion, the pain of the world.

In my own way I was trying to come to terms with the tragic destruction of the Indian people, which seemed so close to the persecution of my own people in the Holocaust of World War II. The so-called Indian Wars were an American Holocaust, which, though they had taken place a century before, still seemed to color the land, soaking it with blood. In a smaller way, I was searching for a way to come to terms with my own broken heart.

———

I tried to take lessons from the knitting of lace, where the contrast of open stitches, forming a sort of absence or negative space, is held in place by solid knitting. You need to have both emptiness and fullness to create the beauty of lace.

Lace appears delicate, but its looks can be deceiving. Working it with the right fiber can create the most durable of fabrics. For my parents' fiftieth wedding anniversary, at my sister's house in Florida, my mother wore a lace pullover made of linen, which I had knitted in London at least three decades before. It looked as good as when I had made it.

Another thing about knitting lace is that when you make a mistake, it's so difficult to rip out and then reconstruct, at least for me, that I have to accept it and move on. Just as in a romantic relationship.

Often when you are knitting a lace or cable pattern, you begin to have an intuitive sense of where certain things go. With lace, for example, there has to be a balance between the number of decreases and yarnovers in a row. You should always end up with the same number of stitches per row. Many lace patterns are circular in nature, with no real beginning or end to the repeats, each motif leading into the next. In the end is the beginning, in the beginning is the end—in the plotting of lace as in the poems of T. S. Eliot's *Four Quartets*.

While knitting lace, if you miss a cue, or when typographically inaccurate directions command you to do something you know doesn't fit with the design (take it from me, it is hell to proofread a knitting pattern), you can trust the internal logic of the pattern, with its predictable rules and changes, to guide your next move. Each row builds upon the row before, as the pattern made by the solid knitting and empty yarnover holes emerges bit by bit. If you pay close attention, you can usually tell where you are.

It took me a long time to learn the lesson that the great knitter Elizabeth Zimmermann used to teach her students—to look at their knitting rather than their printed pattern. I used to be "a blind follower," until a catastrophic mistake I made despite knowing better caused me to adopt a more independent view.

I had been knitting a turquoise chenille cardigan during a trip across the Navajo Reservation in the states around the Four Corners. After I had decreased for and shaped the armholes, after they measured a good nine inches, the instructions told me to knit for a further sixty rows. I followed the pattern and then had to rip out a week's worth of knitting when I got home.

"When you come to a discrepancy between the bird and the book," Audubon used to say, "believe the bird."

If only it were so easy to trust ourselves instead of a reputed higher authority. Unfortunately in my experience, this is a hard-won lesson that takes years to acquire, particularly for women, who are typically taught to defer.

———

There is something about the spaciousness of a huge open vista that alters our inmost psychic landscape. Our perspective changes imperceptibly, as it does when we are confronted with, say, the ceaseless churning of the ocean. I could get that sense of spaciousness, the feeling that I had gone from a small to a very large room, while immersed in my knitting.

Sometimes in meditation I had tried to bring that spaciousness to my feelings about Billy. I sat in pitch-darkness, breathing in and out, until I was inhaling the numberless stars in the vast dome of sky, so that I could bear the earthly heartbreak I knew was to come.

I was trying to cope with loss. The loss of love, the loss of my father, the loss of my hopes, dreams, innocence, and, later, health. The loss of a loved one is a universal human suffering. Sooner or later all of us must deal with illness and death. In that context, it is comforting to contemplate the permanence of the land, the scope of something outside the realm of human comprehension.

Still, loss is loss. And a painful part of the human experience. When the roof of your heart is open to the sky, sometimes the rain gets in.

7. Intimations
of Mortality

KNITTING HELPED ME REPAIR MY RELATIONSHIP WITH MY father and also helped me to complete it.

I'll begin near the end. It is August 2001. I am sitting in my father's room in a hospice facility, where he lies dying. The hospice is a pink stucco building in an old section of Boca Raton, Florida, a place with French doors and balconies, overgrown with giant tropical vines and trees. Though the heat outdoors is stifling, my fingers fashion a dark blue cashmere turtleneck.

It's a pattern I've made before, and simple, so I don't have to think about it. I bought the yarn, which is both soft and substantial, on an impulse at the Knitting Basket. Often once I've completed a sweater, I know how I could make it better the second time, and I do. The pattern for this sweater, which comes from L'Atelier in Santa Monica, has just enough stitch detail in the alternating ribs and solid parts to keep my interest, but not enough to force focused attention. It's perfect for the real work I have to do right now.

Somewhere in my mind I recall a quote, for which I can't locate the source. It says something like "Death came to sit with me and brought her knitting." In my case it's more as if I've come to sit with death and brought my knitting.

It has occurred to me that I am helping to knit my father out of this world. During the previous weeks, when my father knew he was dying but before he lay insensate in this hospice room, I knitted a black wool men's sweater with thick cables that I will probably never wear. But it doesn't seem to matter what I knit, how useless it is or inappropriate for the climate, so long as I just keep knitting.

The quiet motions of my swishing needles and slipping yarn help me sit still and attend this momentous event. It feels as though the thread connects my inner self to the reality now unfolding, which after all is as spiritual as it gets. There is no bigger mystery than life and death. I watch my father metamorphose from his powerful earthly presence to the embryonic being lying silent in the bed. I never knew before how much like birth death is. My father's skin becomes smooth. His thoughts, his feelings, his fears and concerns are as hidden to us as a baby's, his energy focused on the coming transformation.

My whole family is in the room. My cousin who has come down from New York hovers at the metal rail of the hospital bed, grasping my father's unresponsive hand. "Sammy, we're all here," she says. My sister Sheila has a makeshift easel set up in a corner of the room, where she's painting a watercolor. My brother, Ricky, and sister Lorraine have convinced my mother to sing in Yiddish, and she sings song after song, tells jokes and stories, directing her own special brand of Borscht Belt entertainment to her husband of fifty-nine years.

We gather as a family to hold a deathwatch. We're waiting for the patriarch to die.

————

When my father does die, it's in the small hours of the morning, when there's nobody by his side. I am reminded of this months later, when I see the movie *Nowhere in Africa*. One scene strikes me as particularly true. An old tribal woman is dying. Her relatives have moved her out of the family hut into the bush. Jettel, the owner of the farm, demands that she be carried back into the hut so she won't die alone. "She's not alone," says a tribeswoman. "She's with the ancestors."

That was how I felt about my father during the time of his coma, when he seemed to be engaged in some inner work beyond our reach or comprehension.

Because I am staying with my mother and trying to help her through this ordeal, I take her on some necessary errands before we go to sit by the body. My father's face in death is much like his father's, my Papa Joe. His face is his face yet not his face. It is drawn taut over bony features, lacking color and animation. Looking at him, a person I've known all my life, a force to be reckoned with even in decline, alters forever the way I look at life. I know, seeing him, that death really does exist, despite all our best efforts to drive it from our minds, and that inevitably it will come for me.

With my mother and all three of my siblings around, and with other relatives visiting Florida for the funeral and shiva, I think back over my entire relationship with my father. I review our life together as father and daughter: the estrangement of my childhood, the friendship that blossomed in his final years, my fear that he would die, and the reality that he has. Who and what I thought he was, the person he turned out to be, what he gave me, and what he took away.

I'm certain that everyone, staring into the face of a person deeply loved, now dead, asks the same question: Where did he go?

My father was a man of passionate interests, cherished grudges, and longtime resentments, a corrosive bitterness with humans and paradoxical gentleness with nature. Born Goldenberg, he changed his name to Gordon in the 1950s, to combat the anti-Semitism he said kept him from getting jobs. But he remained the same Bronx tough guy, nursing his disgruntlements to the end. "You know us old Goldenbergs," he once told me. "We don't forget nothing."

Now it's gone. A mass of dust. All that's left is the love that endures beyond the grave. That, and a jumble of memories.

Throughout my childhood with my father, I believed I could convince him to love me. Failing that, I could win his respect. I jumped through hoops trying to please him.

I had two great interests in my childhood. One was reading. I was never without a book and couldn't imagine what people did who didn't read constantly. Books were my escape and my salvation. Looking back now, I believe I was actually teaching myself how to write, but I didn't know it then.

My other joy was designing clothes for my paper dolls. I liked the look and texture of different clothing and was extremely involved with touch and feel. Almost my earliest memories are the sensations of different fabrics. I can remember the slink of silk, the smell of fur, the stiff, plush folds of the old-fashioned sofa where I curled my toes as a toddler. I can still conjure up the itchiness of wool skirts that rubbed against my legs, the sashes that pinched my waist too tight. Too young to sew with fiber, I created my own paper dolls, made clothes for them, colored them with crayons, kept them in a special cigar box.

Papa Joe, my grandfather, had a paperweight in the closet of my grandmother's apartment that said, "Clothes maketh the man." He brought me fancy things my parents couldn't afford, riding jodhpurs, a red wool cape, soft leather boots. He dressed impeccably; I always saw him in a suit and a hat.

The lack of love I felt from my father was the great sorrow of my young life. He was a perfectionist, harsh and critical, his weapon a sadistic sarcasm shared by his mother. He was unpredictable and physically violent. All of us children were afraid of his rages.

Both my parents had contempt for women. My father showed his toward my mother, and my mother showed hers through her dearth of women friends or disparaging remarks about the other women in her sphere. She believed that her successful marriage was the crowning achievement of her life and that love was the most important thing that could happen to a woman.

Following my mother's lead, I thought I could fix what had happened to me with my father through my relationships with boys and later men, that I would find someone who would love me as my father had failed to do.

Now I know my perceptions were skewed. When I was a child, I saw as a child. One time in adulthood, almost middle age, I went to Florida to visit my parents. My mother was waiting at the gate for me as I got off the plane. My father was sitting in the waiting area with a newspaper. When he saw me, he broke into a grin so broad and genuine that I knew without doubt he loved me, adored me even.

Following one particularly good visit after we had mended our relationship, he sent me a pair of gold earrings in the mail. I wept as I read the letter that accompanied them. But it was a transforming moment. After that I thought: "I am a woman whose father loves her."

It's true I became a woman whose father loved her. But it is also true that my romantic habits, stirrings of love, thoughts about relationships were formed and developed when I was a girl who believed her father didn't love her. The damage was done. It only helped a little when I realized that my father's difficulty in showing love to his children had more to do with how he felt about himself than how he felt about us.

Later in our lives, when I began going on trips with my father, I sometimes used a meditation technique to place some sort of shield around my heart so I wouldn't absorb the poison of my father's bitterness or share in his resentment toward the people who had wronged him.

As the end grew near, I tried to spend time just sitting with my father on a terrace he had built behind the house. I hoped he would talk to me about his fears of dying, sum up his life, leave me with some profound wisdom that only those at the end of life possess. Instead he went over and over the times he had been slighted, been taken advantage of, undervalued, played for a fool. Even dying, he was full of rage, though a lot of the steam had gone out of it. He was now too tired and frail to be the towering inferno of my youth, his hair-trigger temper toned down to a brittle whisper, his anger barely a threat to me at all.

———

I don't remember when it came to me, some years deep into my recovery, that I wanted to have a relationship with my father. I knew that I would have to be the one to bend. I determined to accept him just the way he was, to go on regular visits to Florida with no agenda of my own, other than being a daughter to my mother and father. I no longer cared if he understood or accepted me, only that I be able to take him at face value for exactly who he was.

My father suffered from congestive heart failure, which is a long, gradual diminishment of powers, punctuated by severe crises and frightening loss of strength and breath. "You know, Gabe," he told my nephew during one of his hospitalizations, "when someone hits you with a truck, they're actually doing you a favor."

I believe that my father, like me, was an essentially lonely person, though he had his consolations. The happiest I ever saw him was when he and my mother lived in a place called Rio Ranches, near Davie, in southwestern Broward County, Florida, during the late 1980s and early 1990s. They lived on a little more than an acre of land. My father had a couple of horses behind the house, along with coops for his racing pigeons. He had ducks, geese, and a pond full of catfish that would eat bread from his hands.

My mother didn't much like it there. "His dream and my nightmare," she called it. It was far from any public transportation, and she had to wait around for my father to take her for groceries, to the library, on her errands to the post office and bank. My parents argued bitterly during this time, something I had never before seen them do. In the past my mother had never disagreed with my father, but apparently that had changed.

My mother felt trapped. Along with the animals in the back, the place had come with a dog named Chase, who sometimes dragged my mother off her feet as she walked him twice a day. Because of the animals' need to be fed, my parents could not take any extended vacations. And my mother was afraid of the creatures. One time she went out to feed them, and a hissing goose cornered her and bit her on the leg. She told everyone in her world—the nearby Publix supermarket and the clinic where my parents received their health care—how the goose had bitten her and turned her leg green.

I thought of this episode as "The goose that ate my mother." It occasioned one of the biggest fights I ever saw my parents have. My mother wanted my father to get rid of the goose.

"It's the goose or me," she shouted.

"I'm not getting rid of nothing," he shouted back.

"You've been married for forty-seven years," I said. "Why do you have to fight like this while I'm here?"

"Don't count on forty-eight," said my father.

One thing I loved about that place in Rio Ranches was that it was close to Seminole tribal headquarters off Sterling Road in Hollywood. I asked my father to take me down to Seminole country because I've always loved their tiny intricate patchwork. Two tribes actually live in that area: the Seminole and the Miccosukee. I believe the Miccosukee were part of the Five Civilized Tribes of the South, which included the Cherokee and the Creek. *Seminole* is a word from another language that means "runaway," and the Seminoles evolved from Indians who fled from the forced relocation of the Trail of Tears and mixed with runaway slaves.

The Seminoles claim that they have never been defeated by the U.S. Army. Soldiers would follow them into the swamps, where their legs would be cut by sawgrass, and the wounds would become infected and fester. Mosquitoes would torment them; the relentless heat drove them mad. In much of South Florida, there's nothing but mangrove, mosquitoes, and heat. "The mangrove silence," Peter Matthiessen calls it in his books about the area.

Sometime in the 1920s missionaries taught the Seminole women how to use sewing machines. The Cowichan peoples of the Pacific Northwest were taught to knit by Scottish missionaries and turned it into an art form of their very own, making heavy waterproof sweaters knitted from yarn spun to the thickness of a finger. The Seminoles mastered the sewing taught them by missionaries and developed a style of doing patchwork that is uniquely theirs and a hallmark of their culture.

I used to think they sewed each tiny piece by hand, but that's not the way it's done. Strips of different colors are sewn together, and then the strips are cut and resewn several times to form geometric patterns. Some of the pieces are fractions of an inch wide. I recently saw a photograph of Pablo Picasso taken sometime in the 1950s in St. Tropez; in it he is wearing a Seminole shirt.

Seminole clothing sold to visitors is priced according to how many strips of patchwork are worked into a garment. The patchwork is interspersed with rickrack and solid stripes of color. In a ceremonial garment worn by a member of the tribe, many strips of patchwork may be used.

The tribe had a trading post in Hollywood, and I told my father to leave me there for a while and go visit one of his friends. I had never seen so much Seminole patchwork in one place; it was hard to choose a single item to buy.

I felt proud when my father came to pick me up and I could introduce him to the women who ran the store. I could see they were pleased to see a father and daughter shopping together, but they weren't half as pleased as I was. I had not spent a lifetime of togetherness with my father, to say the least.

I believe this was the beginning of my father's and my great friendship. From the trading post, we eventually went down to Big Cypress on the Tamiami Trail, and from there we started venturing farther south into the Everglades.

But my father was still my father, still the curmudgeonly tough guy from the Bronx. Once, when I took him to the big Seminole tribal gathering and bought him an Indian taco to eat, he complained about everything: the heartburn he got from the taco; the heat in the bleachers, where we sat to watch the dances; the tourist attractions, such as the caged Florida panther and the alligator wrestling pit. Still, we were there. I had a much better time when I went alone, but I can't recall another time when I took my father to an event like that, so it stands out in my memory.

My father was constantly on the lookout for ripoffs, so we never took an airboat tour in the Everglades; he was convinced that the tour operators had a couple of tame alligators stashed away, kept in place with secret nighttime feedings of chicken. But after our first time to Big Cypress, when we saw baby alligators that had just been hatched pouring out of a gator hole, we saw alligators everywhere we went.

There is a big casino and bingo palace in Big Cypress that I think is not well attended because of its remoteness. My father told me a story about the casino. When the Seminole tribe proposed building it, the state of Florida objected. As it happens, though, part of I-95, the great north-south interstate that runs the length of the Atlantic coast and is the most heavily traveled road in Florida, goes through part of the Seminole reservation.

So the tribe told the state that they wouldn't build their casino; they would simply shut down their section of I-95 and turn it into a toll road to collect revenues for the tribe.

Thus the Big Cypress casino was born.

This illustrated one of my father's favorite precepts: that if you wanted to understand the inner workings of how anything happened, you only had to "follow the buck."

Another of his bywords, which he often told my sister Sheila, was: "If you want to know about people, just watch how animals behave."

———

Rio Ranches was out in what people in Florida call the wild, wild West. There were horse farms in Dania nearby; one local fast-

food restaurant had hitching posts instead of parking spaces for cus-
tomers. My father is buried near that area today, off Griffin Road, in
country that as I write this is still relatively isolated, a place he would
have enjoyed.

In the back of my parents' house was a screened-in pool. At
the time I was still smoking, so my mother set up a little lounge for
me outside, where I could smoke and knit. I always brought knitting
to Florida. When I am knitting, I can withstand boredom, inactivity,
even conversations that would normally make me squirm with rest-
lessness. It is as though I have a little portable world of my own
wherever I go, a haven of refuge and sanity.

My mother has done needlepoint for years, doling out needlepoint pillows among her children and grandchildren like precious
jewels. She also knits, without a pattern, which is nearly incomprehensible to me. She just *potchkes*, as she calls it, fooling around on the
needles until the design comes to her.

While I knitted in the little poolside lounge, my mother
showed me one of the most important lessons of my crafting life,
which was how to make sweaters according to my measurements,
rather than according to the measurements of the printed pattern.
With her help, I made a teal green sweater of mercerized cotton that
I wore for years, one of the best-fitting sweaters I ever produced.

Over the years I did a lot of knitting in Florida and also some
needlepoint. I recall a simple needlepoint design I had, of red gera-
niums with green leaves in a basket set on a black and white checked
tablecloth. The background was lemon yellow, so the canvas had a

bold combination of primary colors in a simplified, stylized design. I remember stitching this canvas for hours as I listened to my father talk about one thing or another. So long as my needlepoint was with me, I was content to listen to whatever he said.

The doctor at my parents' clinic near Rio Ranches had told my mother that my father was a very sick man and could die at any moment. He told her my father wouldn't last for another two years. I remember times at home in California when I was driving my car around the Bay Area and burst into tears because I was afraid my father would die. When I was in Florida, I entered a state of hypervigilance, listening to my father's breathing as he slept, sitting on the edge of my seat in his car, ready at any moment to grab the steering wheel or emergency brake if he began to slump in his seat.

Despite the doctor's predictions, my father lived for another ten years. Even at the end, when he sank into a coma, his damaged heart kept beating long after it should have stopped, so strong was his will to live.

8. Birds
of a Feather

MY FATHER WAS WELL AWARE OF THE PRECARIOUS NAture of his life. Once I asked him why he had become so much nicer and funnier than he used to be. "Getting closer to the man upstairs," he said.

Another time he sent me an antique gold watch he had purchased at an antiques fair in Naples. As he had with the earrings, he sent the watch with a letter that made me weep when I read it. I had to thank my father for the watch on the phone, and I mentioned the letter. "I cried when I read it," I told him, "and I'm afraid I'll cry now on the phone, talking to you about it."

"That's because it's too late now for us to hide anything from each other," my father said. "We have to tell each other the truth."

In his condition, my father should not have been driving, but none of us had the heart to stop him. "You know the old man," he would say. "He likes to be out scouting and patrolling."

My mother found nature "boring" and didn't like to go along with my father on these reconnaissance trips, so I think he was thrilled when I expressed interest in the Everglades and he suddenly had a traveling companion.

We would leave for the Everglades early in the morning, with a cooler full of sandwiches and drinks that my mother packed for us. We went into the park through Homestead, the town reduced to matchsticks by Hurricane Andrew. Its palm trees still are sheared of leaves on the tops, just bare trunks.

In the Everglades National Park we drove south on the road toward Flamingo, stopping at the various turnouts or points of interest to see if we could find any interesting birds. Our trips took place in the winter, February or March. By summer the park was seething with mosquitoes, and though alligators remained behind, all the birds had flown.

In the Everglades we saw purple gallinules, great blue herons, small green herons, egrets, ibises, cranes, ospreys, and peregrine falcons. In Flamingo, at the southernmost tip of the park, we watched huge manatees emerge from the depths of black water like phantoms and encountered rare American crocodiles, with longer, thinner, more dangerous snouts than those of alligators. Alligators were everywhere, lazing in the road where one could easily mistake them for discarded rubber tires, swimming in the pools of the long, shallow river that flowed through the grass.

These trips were always the highlight of my visits to Florida. Of necessity—it took a long time to drive there and back—they usually occurred only once each visit. Because they were peak moments for me, I learned to enjoy them more by expanding the time, stretching it out as it happened as well as in memory. Blocking time, as a knitter rather than a film director might say.

Time is elastic; it expands and contracts. Hence the adage "Time flies when you're having fun" (and drags like a ball and chain when you find yourself trapped and bored). In the mind's eye, time can be manipulated into spaciousness or shrunk into instant passage. I tried to add emptiness to our hours in the Everglades to accommodate more of what I loved, time with my father, time in nature, the big open sky.

This same phenomenon can also be achieved while you knit or do other needlework, as you sink deeply into the eternal present and lose track of passing time.

I believe my father, like me, was greatly consoled by the natural world, the emptiness of the West, the presence of bird and animal life in a richly populated universe.

———

One of the first times I went to Hawaii, I kept changing my return ticket so I could stay for a few more days. "That's the way people move here," a woman I met told me. "They keep changing their tickets, and eventually they never go home."

After a while I realized I would never have enough time in Hawaii, no matter how many times I changed my departure date, so I just bit the bullet and went on home.

That was the way I felt about my father. I knew I could never have enough time with him, so I contented myself with the time I did have and did my best to enjoy it while it was happening. I tried to experience deeply the moments we spent out in nature, adding emptiness to the time, stretching it to make it longer, instead of constantly grasping for more.

————

On one of our trips to the Everglades, after we had been many many times, I told my father we were going to see roseate spoonbills. He scoffed and refused to believe it. Like mine, his cynicism served as a hedge against disappointment. But I turned out to be right.

We got to one of the big ponds near the southern tip of the park at exactly the right time. Giant wood storks picked through the tall grass at the edge of the water, alligators lounged on the banks, great blue and small green herons fished, and two absolutely beautiful roseate spoonbills perched in a tree at the far side of the pond.

After that my father made me an oil painting of a roseate spoonbill standing on one foot in black water. I still have it.

During those years I began talking to my father on the phone.

"I wish you were here, Sue," he said to me one time. "I've been seeing hawks on every telephone pole from here to Okeechobee."

We both were alike in that if we spotted a good bird while driving, we would stop the car and inspect the bird more closely with binoculars. Through our shared love of birds and nature, we forged the sort of relationship I had only dreamed of as a child.

———

It wasn't just me. My father lived long enough to redeem his relationships with all his children, from whom he had been estranged in varying degrees. Toward the end of his life he became interested in computers and began sending us e-mails. I answered him in my customary terse, economical e-mail manner. "From my daughter the writer I expected a few more words," he said.

He and my brother exchanged long, searching e-mails in which Ricky told our father something of his life, his experiences, his concerns. My father also took up oil painting. My sister Sheila is a portrait and landscape painter, and my father used to go to her studio and discuss technique with her. He also grew close to Lorraine and came to value her massages and healing potions.

About a year before he died, my father experienced cardiac arrhythmia. He went into full cardiac arrest, in hospital parlance, a code blue, or a medically confirmed death. During this experience he told us he saw his mother coming for him with her arms outstretched, but the doctors jabbed IVs into both his arms and brought him back to life.

This was the life-threatening emergency Sheila called me about when Billy left me for Louise. It was a scary time, but we all pulled together, and somehow my father got through it and eked out another year of life.

When he got out of the hospital, I took him to Loxahatchee in his van. Loxahatchee is a small park in the northern part of the Everglades. It is in Boca Raton, near where my sister lives. By that time my parents had moved to Delray Beach, which is close by.

Loxahatchee is like a tiny taste of the Everglades, all waving grass and empty sky with some alligators in the ponds and waterbirds picking their way through the shallows.

As we approached our parking space, an osprey holding a fish in its talons flew right by the windshield, and my father and I exclaimed in unison, "Ahhh!"

My father remained fragile through the last year of his life. He also began having difficulty sleeping and stayed awake most of the night, with my worried mother sitting up with him to make sure he didn't fall when he walked around the house.

I later found out these sleepless episodes, called sundowners, are common to the dying. It was only after we had gotten my father out of intensive care and into hospice care near the end that he began sleeping again.

"I've made my decision," he said then. "And now I can have some peace."

One thing I inherited from both my parents is good hands.

In the years we lived on Long Island, from 1952 to long after I was grown, I watched my father work with his hands. He was a do-it-yourselfer. He had grown up poor, was handy by nature, and had learned in his life to build or fix whatever he wanted. Though I was a lazy and resentful child, I watched and often helped him dig gardens, build retaining walls, construct dormers, add bathrooms, plaster and wallpaper rooms. He was a man of hobbies and intensely consuming interests, and he worked with quiet concentration and obsessive perfectionism.

Sometimes I wonder how he felt at the end of his life as congestive heart failure sapped his powers and his strength. He had been a strong and formidable man. I can remember him hanging off the roof, dressed in a white T-shirt and khaki pants, hammer in his hand, building a dormer window for my parents' bedroom.

I watched him make his own fishing poles. He wound the colored thread around guide hooks for the fishing line in patterns of stripes and then added varnish to finish and waterproof the thread. He painted his fish tanks with a magical sort of paint that formed geometric crystals I later saw frost form on my windows in Minneapolis. He caulked boats and painted signs and did perfect renditions of his paint-by-number kits, and I, his quiet, sulky, and ever-watchful child, observed.

My mother and father took lessons and became expert Latin dancers. My father would come home from work on a Friday evening and take a long nap. Around ten or so my parents got dressed to go out to one of the beach clubs in Long Beach. My mother had a sequined low-cut red dress she sometimes wore, and my father, who had grown his sideburns long and tried a comb-over in the fashions of the seventies, wore a ruffled light blue shirt. Off they would go to mambo, cha-cha, or rumba the night away in synchronized harmony.

My father worked hard and played hard. He had rhythm in his body and skill in his hands.

———

I'm pleased to take after my father. I find, as I found as a child, a delicious pleasure in what I feel and fashion with my hands. The world of color, of fiber, of yarn and thread continues to engage me.

Even the sorts of political action I favor sometimes involve thread.

My friend Norman Kennedy, the Scottish folksinger and master weaver, once told me that women cast their spells in Scotland by arranging red yarn in a pattern on the ground. In the Pacific Northwest something called yarning is used to still the chain saws of clear-cut logging. Instead of spiking a tree or lying down in front of a bulldozer, someone winds yarn among the trees. The yarn gets into the innards of a chain saw and disables the machinery, without causing damage to logger or tree.

The way I see it, there is precious little left of the world's great beauty, and it is up to us to preserve it however we can.

Norman, who is such a skilled handspinner that someone once watching him spin accused him of being "an alien," claims that knitting and spinning are empowering skills to those who learn them. Most people, he says, don't know they can make things for themselves without going to buy them in a shop.

In Norman's world, knitting ties in with birds. Girls in the Shetland Islands, he once told me, learn to knit on the spines of seagull feathers that have been stripped of the feathery parts. The girls must learn the proper tension. If they grasp the knitting too tightly, the seagull feathers collapse. If they grasp it too loosely, the feathers fail to hold the yarn. Once the girls have learned how to knit on the feathers, they are allowed to progress to wires or needles.

In my inner life too, birds and knitting go together. Many aboriginal peoples view birds as intermediaries between heaven and earth. Knitting keeps us grounded on the earth as our minds and spirits soar through the heavens. It's all a part of the natural world. My father feeding bread to catfish in the pond on his land in Rio Ranches. Both of us watching with binoculars as raptors circle in the skies. Sheep rambling through briars and brambles, growing thick woolly coats to be spun into yarn and knit into garments on the spines of seagull feathers. Everything all of a piece.

————

Bodies of water hold a magic for me. "Women gather power from walking by the water," Deb Fuller, an Ojibway Indian and friend of Judycarol's and mine in Minnesota, always says.

For most of my family's life together, we lived close to the water. My parents owned a boatyard for thirty years. It fronted onto

Reynolds Channel, one of the feeder channels on the South Shore of Long Island that empties into the Atlantic Ocean, less than thirty minutes away.

I think of our lives on that body of water. Our own bodies, our human bodies, the ones the mystics tell us are difficult to come by and a precious opportunity for evolution, are made up primarily of water.

Our blood is made up of water and carries our emotions. Our ties to one another, the love that survives death, the precious love between parent and child, husband and wife, brother and sister, friend to friend, all that is carried by the water in our bodies.

When something touches us deeply or wounds us to the quick, we cry tears of salt water, with a composition similar to the ocean, indistinguishable from the seas. As babies in the womb we float in a sea of amniotic fluid, salty water that cushions us as we grow.

All the years I was troubled in my addiction, I could always return to the boatyard for healing and strength. The consoling presence of water and light restored me to nominal health and a semblance of sanity.

I gravitate toward bodies of water. When I've been away from it too long, I crave the ocean, the sound of the waves, the breathing in and out of the big body, the body that contains us all.

The water in Hawaii has been a conduit of bliss for me. It travels thousands of miles without touching another body of land, so it is as pure as it's going to get when it laps against the shores of the islands. I've watched in silent awe the close presence of humpback whales in that water, heard their enormous *whoosh* as they dive into the sea. I've stood in water on a deserted beach and experienced a wave of tiny silver fish leaping out of the water and back down exactly where I was, close enough to tickle my legs.

In the last year of my father's life I sometimes immersed myself in the Atlantic Ocean so I could bear what was going to happen. This was during the time my father found it difficult to sleep. He once told me Sheila had made him a bed on one of her couches and he enjoyed a slumber that was "silky, like Arabian nights."

In his last weeks he liked to be taken to a fishing hole in Boynton Beach, Florida. Over the years he had made some friends there, and he enjoyed talking with them in the evening. There were boats going in and out of the harbor, waves crashing along the pilings of the cove, the smells of bait and fish, the cries of seagulls and the sight of them wheeling in the air. I think my father liked the fishing hole because it reminded him of the place on Long Island where we had lived.

It was tricky taking my father anywhere at that point. He resisted all the apparatus that accompanied his infirmity. He didn't like us to take along his oxygen when we went out, wouldn't use the walker the hospice workers had provided him with, railed against the hospital bed in the house.

At home, he often fell. His legs would go out from under him, and he would tumble to the ground. One night, when my brother and I took our parents to the fishing hole, my father fell while walking from the car to the bench. It was difficult to pick him up, even more difficult to see the shocked and vulnerable expression on his face at the realization of his own frailty.

I heard my father tell his oldest friend he was going "to the place from which no man returns." He knew he was at the end of his life and was struggling to accept it. I think about my father as I myself struggle to accept the unacceptable: the fact that everybody dies.

———

In the last place my parents lived, my father kept his tools in a big closet in the bedroom. This was much diminished from the large collection that had once required a huge storage shed to contain them. My father had a low bench in the closet, and he sat on it while he went through his tools.

Because Billy, my former boyfriend, was a construction guy, like my father, they had sometimes talked to each other on the phone. My father was looking for some tools to give Billy, "as a personal gift from me, in hopes he'll straighten out."

For some reason he had been talking about chronometers. I didn't know what a chronometer was, but I liked the sound of the word and the way it rolled around in my mouth. So I may have asked about a chronometer.

My father sat low to the ground on his bench and went through each tool in his heavy toolbox. It was getting late in the evening, and my mother was exhausted. She wanted to go to bed.

Each night, when my father got into bed, she sponged and pow-
dered him, and then he fell asleep.

"Come on," she said, "I can hardly stand up anymore."

"OK, Dad," I said. "Go to bed. You can do that tomorrow."

My father became annoyed. "Just a minute," he said. "I'm saying good-bye to my tools. Do you think this is easy?"

I caught my breath. When my uncle Lou died, his sons had
spoons carved on his tombstone because he loved to play the
spoons. When Sheila from the Knitting Basket died, her daughter
Nuala put needles and yarn in her casket because she could not bear
to think of her mother alone in the afterlife with nothing to knit. My
father, who had been a builder and worked with tools his whole life,
was contemplating a future without his beloved tools.

The Christmas after my father died, I was shopping and came
across a tiny toolbox with miniature tools in it, something you might
find in a dollhouse. I bought it and placed it close to his picture, as
a sort of offering to his spirit.

———

On one of the last nights I ever spent in the same house with
my father, the *Godfather* series was playing on TV. My father had become fairly deaf by then, and the volume on the TV was so loud that
when the gangsters opened fire, it sounded as if they were shooting
in my bedroom. That sad and majestic music was playing all night.
Dum da da dum, da da da. Dum da da dum, da da da. A sound
track for epic tragedy.

I had made up my mind to go home to California. Though we knew my father was dying, we didn't know if it would be days, weeks, or months before he did. That night I knew I was leaving in the morning and might never see him alive again.

I went to say goodnight to my father. As I bent down to kiss him, the air between us was so heavy and thick with feeling you almost could touch it with your hand. I didn't want to break down in front of him, and I guess he felt the same. The feeling without words between us was one of the most profound emotions I've ever experienced.

Those last moments were so unbearable for my father and me, so filled with bottomless sadness and grief that we couldn't even speak our minds in words. We had to speak from our hearts and through our eyes. The words were about nothing but Brooklyn.

I think I expected him to say something meaningful to me, something deep and soulful and pithy, words to remember.

The television played in the background and must have captured my father's attention. It was an ad for a documentary about Brooklyn. Suddenly my father said to me, "You know, Sue, Brooklyn is a very interesting borough. It was settled four hundred years before the Bronx."

So in one of life's little ironies, those might be his final words to me, while all that we thought, feared, and felt about each other would hang in the air unsaid. That was life, and I suppose it was also death.

As my plane neared the Bay Area, I broke down in tears. I was sure that my father had died while I was in flight and that it had been a terrible mistake to leave.

I called Florida the minute I walked in the door. My father answered the phone. "How did you like the *Godfather* movies?" I asked him after we had said our hellos. "I don't know," he said. "You and your mom made me have the TV so low, I couldn't even hear them."

By the time I returned to Florida, my father had been moved from home to the hospice facility, and there were no more conversations to be had.

———

Years of spiritual study have done little to diminish the mystery of death for me, though meditation has strengthened my belief in reincarnation, in the endless recycling of souls through time, in the existence of a grand design in which each of us plays a part.

Several months after my father died, I heard that my niece Maggie, who lives in Australia, was pregnant with her third child. I wondered if the child might contain the spirit of my father. Maggie was always a favorite of his, and he would have welcomed the chance to grow up in a land as foreign as Australia.

We can speculate all we want, but nobody really knows, except, possibly, the highest of Tibetan lamas. I may be certain that reincarnation exists, but I have no idea how it works, the mechanics of it, whether it is as direct as the transmigration of the soul from one earthly body to another.

Nevertheless, I did what I know how to do. I started knitting a sweater for Maggie's baby. I combined two yarns, a soft blue cotton and a beaded cotton hand-painted in shades of magenta, orange, and green. I made the sweater in a pattern I liked, a heavy cardigan with a hood.

I felt a lot of tenderness toward that baby, mixed with tenderness toward my father. I finished the sweater with buttons in the shape of fish. Then I held it against my body, as though I were holding the baby inside it, as though I were hugging my father.

I mailed the sweater to Australia. When it came in the mail, my great-nephew Dominick, Maggie's oldest, said, "Look, Mummy, the buttons look like fish. Won't the new baby just love that?"

9. Silence Is the Best Remedy

WE BURIED MY FATHER IN A LUSH FIELD OF GREEN to the west of Pembroke Pines in a place called Menorah Gardens. He had shown me the cemetery when we were out on a drive, just as he repeated to Sheila the details of what he wanted for his funeral: the Masons performing a ceremony; a color guard of Jewish War Veterans; a live bugler playing "Taps."

A soft rain, what the Navajo call a female rain, was falling, and in the distance, almost to the woods at the end of the field, dragonflies and purple martins flitted over the grass. It lifted my heart to see wings in such abundance, their presence life-affirming and spiritual. I knitted those wings into my blue sweater too.

I appreciated every one of the people who

showed up for the actual burial, an hour and a half away from the funeral home. The rabbi said it was a mitzvah, a selfless act for the benefit of another, to throw a shovelful of dirt on the coffin, to help bury the dead.

During the funeral Ricky and I both read poems we had written about my father. Mine was titled "Emperor of the Birds" and described my father amid the birds and animals of his little ranch. Ricky's was about our dad's fascination with cowboy movies and all things western. Lorraine read a song she had written about our parents' great love affair, which had lasted close to sixty years.

She also read a poem her daughter Maggie had e-mailed. It ended with an image of my father tipping his baseball cap, flashing his wide grin, and riding off into the great unknown on his horse.

I found great comfort in the rituals of the funeral and in the burial itself and thought back over them for months afterward.

I also thought a lot about my father. He was known to have some strange opinions. One of them was that following the end of World War II "they should have given the Jews the Bronx." He would sometimes follow pronouncements such as these with the coda "I have spoken," like an old-time orator or Native American chief.

The day my father died I took my mother to do errands. One of her tasks was to bring my father's clothes to the funeral home. She managed to forget to provide him with pants.

This omission went into our family mythology, along with the strangeness of my cousin Carole's driving ten blocks backward on busy Federal Highway, with Ricky in the car.

During the week preceding my father's death, my siblings and I gathered at Sheila's house and told stories of our father, many concerning how much we'd been frightened of him when we were young.

I'd been the eldest and received, along with Lorraine, his attempts to control us and turn us into a reflection of the image he wished to present in the world. But Ricky had been the only child still living at home after all the sisters had married or left.

Ricky had both the benefits and disadvantages of being the only boy, the advantage being a sort of regard that we girls never had, the disadvantage being the expectation that he could perform hard physical tasks because he was a boy.

He told a story about being assigned to shovel a whole pile of concrete blocks into place on a day when he had tickets for the opera with his friends. He ran away to Sheila's house. When he called home to see how mad my father was, my mother said he'd better get home and shovel those blocks before another day went by.

———

My mother, who has little regard for religious observance, went through the funeral and shiva all right. But she didn't want to visit the cemetery and didn't plan a traditional unveiling of the tombstone, a year from the day of death. She never even ordered the stone. After Sheila and I had visited our father's unmarked grave, we ordered the stone ourselves.

Menorah Gardens by this time had been the subject of many

scandals. It was said that some of its plots were no better than swamps, with coffins floating around in the muck, and that it had been stacking up bodies, burying people one on top of the other. This was not true of the place where my father was buried, and Sheila said it would have been a great comfort to him to know his coffin was safe.

In Jewish tradition, it is customary to leave a small pebble when you visit a grave. For some reason, there are no pebbles or rocks to be found at Menorah Gardens, so Sheila and I brought decorative pebbles from her house. We went to the cemetery on what would have been my father's birthday, got our first look at the stone, a flat granite block set flush with the ground, inscribed with the Star of David and Masonic symbols, and had a good cry.

Then, as we knelt near the stone, something came over me. "Dad," I said, "Mom's driving us crazy." Both Sheila and I went from tears to sudden, hysterical laughter.

"He said, 'What did I tell you?' " I told Sheila. " 'Now do you believe me?' "

I didn't actually feel that my father was there in the cemetery, but I was glad we visited the gravesite as a gesture of respect. It reminded me of the poem sometimes said at funerals: "Do not stand at my grave and weep; I am not there; I do not sleep."

The pebble I had taken from Sheila's was an iridescent glass stone. I placed it on a corner of the headstone. Sheila's pebble was bright blue and was on the opposite corner.

After we had been at the gravesite for a while, we stood up simultaneously and walked away from the plot. I turned back to look. The iridescent glass pebbles glinted in the sun.

———

After my father died, it occurred to me that for the past ten years or so, I had never gone to Florida without a black dress in my suitcase in case I needed it for a funeral. Every time the phone rang early in the morning or late at night when I was at home, I assumed it was emergency news about my father. I had figuratively sat on the edge of my seat, expecting the worst, for well over a decade.

There is a certain type of peacefulness that settles over you after something you've feared for a long time has finally come to pass. I grieved hard for my father, but I noticed too the absence of a familiar panic that had hung around at the edges of my mind for years, the fear of his imminent death.

I was grateful I had taken the time to forge a bond with him. Though I missed him every day, I was happy that he had lived long enough for us to develop a friendship and that I had found within myself the willingness to simply be his daughter.

While my father was still at home, being cared for by hospice, I had been knitting a black wool sweater with large cables. It was just something to knit. A way to live through what was happening, unconsciously to record it in the fiber of the yarn. I can't bring myself to part from that sweater. It holds the record of my father's last days with me, the bittersweet memories of knowing you are sharing the end of a bond with a person you deeply love.

When I came back from California, and my father was in the hospice facility, I was making the navy blue cashmere pullover. I knitted it the whole time my father was in the hospice. I may even have been knitting at the funeral. I can't recall.

In Arica, my spiritual school, we have a ceremony we do for a person after he or she has died. I did the ceremony for my father in Big Sur, with some old-time Aricans, one of whom had known my family. We were in the home of one of the women, high up on Pfeiffer Ridge, above the fog, with a splendid view of the Santa Lucia Mountains. The other Aricans in the room say that they saw a lot of light during the ceremony and that my father seemed at peace.

I had a vision of my father riding his horse over the magnificent mountains. He would have loved the wild beauty of Big Sur. I felt the ceremony was a fitting tribute to him.

I finished the navy blue sweater during that time in Big Sur. I sewed it together in the house. Of all the sweaters I have made, this is the one I wear the most. It is not the most beautiful, or the softest, or the best fitting. But it is so filled with meaning, with the tenderness of those last days, that I derive immense comfort from wearing it. It is almost as if it and the black sweater I knitted close to the end hold some of my father's spirit.

I received the gift of real solitude while grieving my father's death. I spent a lot of time by myself, quietly at night, watching TV and knitting. I didn't want to go out or to speak to people. I cried when the urge to cry came upon me. I didn't try to run from my sadness or ignore the fact that it was happening. I just embraced it and went with the flow of feeling.

During this time I watched a lot of westerns. I watched the HBO series *Band of Brothers*, about a company of American soldiers during World War II. I felt close to my father while watching John Wayne, a great favorite of his, or programs on the History Channel about the war he had fought in. Even the very act of watching TV, something I hadn't much done in my life, reminded me of my father.

My mother too began watching TV. As she said, "For almost sixty years I could never watch what I wanted." She began watching reruns of *The Golden Girls, Designing Women*, films for women on the Lifetime channel. "I'm also getting to see the ends of all the movies your father walked out of," she said. When I stayed with her in Florida, I sometimes heard her laughing in the living room at the antics of the Golden Girls, the tart comments of Estelle Getty, who, as my mother observed, always wore a hand-knit sweater.

My mother and I had gone to see the movie *Captain Corelli's Mandolin* together. It wasn't a particularly entertaining movie, but both of us noticed that all the girls on the Greek island wore hand-knit sweaters. "They had to," my mother said. "They couldn't go to Bloomingdale's to buy them."

During the time I was mourning my father, some of my friends thought I was depressed and should consider going on antidepressant medication. I wasn't depressed, I was grieving. There's a difference. In my mind, grief is completely appropriate, a sublimely honoring and human emotion.

In her book *Refuge,* written while her mother was dying of cancer and the rise of the Great Salt Lake was destroying a bird refuge she loved, Terry Tempest Williams quotes Thomas Merton. "Silence is the strength of our interior life..." he writes. "If we fill our lives with silence, then we will live in hope..."

Silence is a natural companion to knitting, though the craft can also be performed in groups, like the knitting circles that are currently popular. Lace is just demanding enough that one's attention cannot stray too far from the counting and repetitions of the pattern without making a mistake, but not so demanding as to require total focus and attention.

In the workshops I sometimes led at Esalen, I alternated periods of knitting in silence with group discussions of such topics as harmony and grace. I learned the format for the silent needlework from Sylvia Boorstein's book about Vipassana Buddhist meditation, *It's Easier Than You Think*. Over the course of a weekend, if everything went well, the quality of the silence deepened, and the group cohered into a larger whole.

Knitting in a group encourages socializing, along with the sharing of tips and techniques. When practiced alone, in silence, it encourages soul-searching, deep exploration of the knitter's inner world. It is the perfect vehicle for both terrains, the open vistas of the internal world, and the nourishing community of like-minded women engaged in a productive, absorbing activity of the hands.

My experience knitting the various versions of the Kerry Blue Shawl during my affair with Billy had taught me an appreciation of the shawl form. Shawls tend to be large, meaning that once engaged in knitting a shawl, the knitter can look forward to a long period of uninterrupted knitting. Shawls need neither shaping nor decisions about fit, so the knitting can be steady and rhythmical. Though I rarely wore the shawls I made, I enjoyed making them; they fitted my criteria for pieces of knitting as art projects.

I knitted several shawls from Cheryl Oberle's book *Folk Shawls*, which is full of wonderful patterns and stories. Whenever I could afford them, I bought cones of pashmina, a term that refers to cashmere from India, not to the cashmere-silk blend of the garments called pashminas, by mail order from Joseph Galler. The pashmina is soft, slippery, lustrous, and luxurious in the extreme. I used a pearl gray pashmina to make the Bird's Nest Shawl in Oberle's book and also did a version of the Wool Peddler's Shawl in brilliant red and a tricolor triangle of Icelandic origin in black, brown, and ecru.

The Icelandic shawl, though not my favorite to knit, has become my favorite to wear. It slips easily over whatever nightclothes I wear in the winter, large enough to provide warmth, light enough to feel weightless, dark enough to disappear from sight.

Cheryl's story of the Bird's Nest Shawl is particularly engaging. In the Himalayan Mountains between India and Tibet, cashmere goats wandering along trails leave bits of fleece on bushes as they pass. Birds then collect the fleece and use it to line their nests. Once the nests have been abandoned, poor men of the local villages gather the bits of cashmere and give it to their wives to spin into yarn to be used for weaving prayer shawls.

I liked the story and the pleasing look of the shawl, a large rectangle with single and double bands of lace alternating at intervals. The tricky part about rectangular shawls is that the cast on and cast off have to be loose enough that the shawl's borders drape freely. In my first try at the shawl, I failed to do the borders properly, so I made it again, with improvements the second time.

I ordered yarn from Cashmere America, a collective based in Sonora, Texas. This cashmere has a rougher finish than the slinky pashmina and comes in only two colors, natural and light brown. I ordered a fine yarn in the darker color and knitted it double. The finished shawl has a comforting weight and heft to it and is large and enveloping, the way that a prayer shawl is meant to be.

I knitted the second Bird's Nest Shawl over a long period of time, perhaps several months. The lace was a simple repeat, and because I was familiar with the pattern, I could do it while watching television. During this time there was a history of jazz in installments that aired over public TV at about ten at night.

I watched the jazz show, listened to the music, and knitted long rows of rough cashmere. I was sad during this time, actively grieving, but the combination of the lace and the jazz fell into a natural rhythm and provided me with a contentment as deep and satisfying as any I have known.

There was a richness to these nights of knitting and jazz that reminded me of how I had felt while pregnant with my daughter. I had a sense of sadness but also a sense of grace. A feeling of becoming, a moment of drifting seamlessly with time. It's all contained in the Bird's Nest Shawl, which wraps around like a gift of silence, the manifestation of wordless prayers echoing through the formless void.

10. Intertwining

I SOMETIMES THOUGHT THAT THE MAGICAL QUALITIES I ascribed to my knitting were figments of my imagination; then something would happen that I couldn't explain.

In November 2002, the day after Thanksgiving, Judith, one of my oldest and dearest friends, committed suicide. She shot herself in the head with a gun no one even knew or suspected she had in her possession. The particular method, employed by a committed pacifist, and the timing, after she had bought a dress and sent out invitations for her annual fancy holiday party, came as a profound shock to all in her sphere.

Judith had been despondent, and seriously beyond even severe depression, for about twelve years before she took her life. I believe she suffered from some form of mental illness; whether it was bipolar disorder or schizophrenia or psychosis, I don't know. She had breaks with ordinary reality that I sometimes thought might be a spiritual rather than a psychological problem and was badly served by the professionals to whom she turned for help.

Oddly, she had appeared to be improving for the two years or so before her suicide. But two months previous to her death, she had taken me out to dinner and said in the course of our conversation that she didn't want to live anymore. In retrospect, it seemed that she had been trying to say good-bye.

Judith and her husband, Ray, a university professor, had a close-knit group of friends with whom they socialized on a regular basis. Judith had birthday parties for herself and for Ray, with whom I shared a birth date, as well as holiday parties, Thanksgiving dinners, anniversary celebrations, Easter egg hunts for children, Buddhist meditation events, and various fund-raisers and dinner parties. I was one of her oldest friends, having known her in college. Judith and Ray's parties were so warm, with such a good feeling to them, that you couldn't help becoming friends with their other friends and family.

They were also splendid and elegant affairs, with catering by Chez Panisse regulars and beautiful clothes, including a gauzy silk Venetian gown hand-painted with roses that Judith wore one year and that was among the most beautiful dresses I have ever seen.

About a month before Judith died, my friend Marilyn Rinzler, whom I met at one of Judith's Thanksgivings, went with Judith and me to see the movie *Frida*. It was the cinematic life story of the Mexican artist Frida Kahlo, the great painter of jewellike self-portraits, who endured a life of unimaginable physical torment before dying at age forty-seven. "I hope the end is peaceful and I hope never to return," she wrote in her journal. I wonder now what went through Judith's mind as she read those words on the screen.

I also thought in the succeeding months about Frida's painting of her friend who committed suicide by jumping out a window of the Plaza Hotel. Was that suicide as incomprehensible to Frida as Judith's was to us? Did she paint to make sense of it herself?

Like Frida, Judith was a tormented soul, as tortured in her way as any martyred Catholic saint. She was serious, earnest, and capable of rapturous mystical experiences when the world would crack open and she would glimpse its heartbreaking beauty. Whether her torment was emotional, physical, or spiritual, it became unendurable to her, and for all the years that I knew her, I never glimpsed the secret places to which she went when her grip on reality gave way to psychosis and formless terror.

In the grief I experienced following her death, I found comfort only in the moments of tenderness I had managed to show her when she was alive. She was so vulnerable that at times I treated her as tenderly as a child. In the midst of dinner at a restaurant, for example, she would suddenly begin sobbing inconsolably, and all I could do was hold her hand and sit patiently with her until the storm of tears had passed.

She was a kind and compassionate person and exceedingly generous. I believe that everyone who knew her and every organization she involved herself in benefited in some way from her largess.

One year, for her birthday, which fell around Memorial Day, I took her out to lunch at a restaurant I liked near Jack London Square and presented her with a woolen sweater I had knitted for her. The sweater was a Jo Sharp design, striped in subtle gradations from gray to pumpkin to magenta to purple. I had modified the pattern, adding pockets, as I usually did, and had found the perfect dark red buttons with a wood grain pattern that showed through the stain. I was pleased to be able to give her such a splendid gift, and she was happy to receive it.

She wrote me that the sweater reposed in state in her house and that everyone who came to visit had to experience a viewing of "the sweater." She also told me that she took it on a trip to London and it kept her warm through a damp English springtime.

When I found out Judith had died, I wondered about the sweater. I almost wished for the sweater to accompany her on her journey to the spirit world, or wherever it is we go after we die. But that was not to be.

A few days after her death there was a small memorial service for Judith in the garden of her home. Judith's sister, Bettina, was there. Bettina resembled Judith so closely, not only in her countenance but in gestures and facial expressions and even the way she crossed her legs, that seeing her was almost uncanny. I had met Bettina before and seen her occasionally over the years, but this time was different, fraught with searing pain.

Alone among people she knew, Judith had called to leave Bettina a message on her answering machine before she picked up the gun, albeit with the knowledge that her sister was away from home.

"Good-bye," she said. "I love you."

I of course brought my knitting to the memorial service with me. I was working on some hand-dyed merino tape that had spots of jewel-bright color on a ground of midnight blue. The yarn was the shape of raw-edged fettuccini; its colorway had been named Venezia, one of the reasons I'd bought it. When I went to pay my condolences to Bettina, she asked to see the knitting from my bag.

"Maybe I'll commission something from you," she said.

"I'm not very good at commissions," I said, "but I did knit Judith a sweater, and I'd love for you to have it."

We decided to get it right then and there and, although there was a crush of people waiting to speak to her, managed to maneuver our way through the crowd and up the winding staircase almost as though we were invisible. We arrived at Judith's bedroom and opened her closets. I pointed out the sweater to Bettina. It had been freshly cleaned; its double cuffs were folded open.

"Oh," said Bettina. "I saw that one and wanted to take it. She wore that a lot."

"I loved her so much," I blurted out to Bettina, overcome with emotion. "I can't think of anyone I'd rather have that sweater than you."

It was late afternoon and growing chilly, as it does in the Bay Area when the fog rolls in. Bettina took the sweater, folded up the cuffs, and put it on over her black dress.

She wore it for the duration of the service. I hope she was comforted by its warmth and the love in the stitches intended for her sister. I was comforted by seeing her in it and felt honored that she had chosen to wear it. Though Judith possessed closets full of clothing, dating back decades of her life, there was something so intimate about the sweater I had made for her by hand that it couldn't help lending an air of intimacy and warmth to the wearer.

I told a small sort of funny story at the service. I had met Judith in college, more than forty years before. Our paths had crossed and recrossed with our trips across the country. I was already living in Berkeley when she moved there with Ray. She was still living here when I came back after having been gone for fourteen years.

Shortly after I returned in 1988, I attended a reading at Black Oak Books. I can't remember who was reading, but it was a popular event, and the store was packed with people. I heard someone call my name and looked around. Judith was sitting underneath a table, cross-legged on the floor.

"Look, Susan," she said to me, "I saved you a seat."

For some reason, out of all the times we had shared, that one stood out for me as a Judith moment, something that illustrated her sly sense of humor and mischief, the way she could sometimes make something from nothing.

I couldn't help wondering, as I watched Bettina trying to express her feelings of loss and devastation, how I would feel if it had been one of my sisters who was gone and I had been unable to save her from despair.

There is no doubt that great love occasions great pain when the object of that love is gone. Our grief is a measure of the love we feel, the depths of our caring and the softness of our souls. I wanted to cry out, as Nell cries out at the end of Toni Morrison's *Sula*, "We was girls together."

I remembered the first time I saw Judith. She was rushing down the corridor of our college dorm with her toothbrush in her hand. "I can't stop to talk," she said. "I only have three minutes to brush my teeth."

We were the most unlikely pair you could imagine being destined to remain friends for a lifetime. She was the top student in our class, I barely went to classes. She was wealthy; I was poor. She was motivated; I was slovenly.

I can't even remember what created our bond. I recall going down to New York with Judith's grandmother Gagi in a chauffeur-driven Bentley with robes across our laps. I recall Judith's being expelled from school after she'd taken an engagement ring from the room of one of our classmates. Like her suicide by gunshot forty years later, it was an action no one who knew her could associate with the person they knew. In years to come, she referred to it as her first psychotic break.

Perhaps we remained friends because we both lived in Berkeley. My daughter and I became part of her extended family. During a time of temporary emotional distress for my daughter, Judith knew she was in trouble before I did, because her own personal anguish made her attuned to the sufferings of others.

Sometime in the 1980s I went to the movies with Judith and Ray. As we walked through downtown Berkeley, every homeless person on the street called out to Judith by name, because she worked with each of them individually. She worked with children, with conscientious objectors, with refugees from war-torn parts of the world, with torture victims and women who had struggled to survive.

In college some of the few Jewish girls in our class would get together and wonder: "Who would hide you from the Nazis?" I believe Judith was one of the few who would have, so great were her compassion and degree of moral outrage about injustices toward others.

In the end she could help everyone, but she couldn't help herself. I remember running into her hurrying through City Center Plaza in downtown Oakland one day. She was setting up a table to talk to people about the American flag in the wake of September 11. "What does the flag mean to you?" was the question she and her meditation partner posed to the public. I hadn't expected to see her there, but I will always be grateful that when I did, I kissed her full on the lips.

I knitted on the Venezia sweater during the memorial service, though Marilyn reached out to still my hands during one particularly solemn moment. To go with the sweater, I bought handmade glass buttons, fused glass with an inner fuchsia color that rose from depths of blue. Sometimes I name my sweaters, and I thought of this one as "Judith in Italy," where she went every summer.

I showed the finished work to Bettina when she returned to Berkeley to pick up some of Judith's things. I wanted to give it to her as a gift, but she insisted on paying me for it. The note she wrote me afterward had a stylized scene of Venice on the front.

I had harbored a fantasy of going to Venice. I didn't actually get there, at least not yet. But I visited the Venice of my imagination while I was knitting that sweater, its deep blues, roses, and burnished Renaissance tones recalling the splendor of the water city's palazzos, gondolas, and canals.

I'm glad Bettina has that sweater now. I feel that it knits us together forever, Judith, Bettina, and me.

11. Testing Limits of Earth and Sky

December 2002

I HAVE BREAST CANCER. IT SEEMED TO HAPPEN ALL AT once, but of course that's not exactly true.

Six months or so ago I noticed a slight redness on the skin of one of my breasts. I had just read a newspaper article about several women who worked in the same office and who had come down with inflammatory breast cancer that began with redness on the skin. But I didn't go to the doctor. The hamster wheel of my newspaper job, the demands of having to come up with three distinct ideas for columns each week and then research and write them, took precedence over my health.

"Maybe it will go away," I thought. It didn't. Somehow I had managed to convince myself that I would never get breast cancer, though I grew up in the cancer cluster of Nassau County, Long Island, and live in the breast cancer capital of the United States, the San Francisco Bay Area.

Thirty years ago I had a biopsy on a large fibroid cyst in my right breast following a bad cancer scare. It turned out to be benign. Because I was used to feeling lumps and bumps, I didn't become unduly alarmed when my breast began to feel lumpier.

But of course I knew. On some level I knew. I remember the precise feeling I had one day in the shower while soaping that breast, knowing something wasn't right, being too frightened or too much in denial to do something about it.

One day the skin that had been red began to feel peculiar, thicker somehow, like scar tissue, like skin with a keloid scar. I tried to convince myself that it was scar tissue from the old breast biopsy.

I hadn't had a mammogram in four years.

I ate cancer-crunching cruciferous vegetables, had acupuncture, practiced homeopathy, took nutritional supplements, lost weight. To top it all off, I had had one form of cancer already.

I felt the strange skin on a Friday. The advice nurse at Kaiser, my HMO, told me to call on Monday for a same-day appointment. I put it out of my mind for the weekend, called Monday morning, and went in Monday afternoon. The nurse practitioner gave me a breast exam and got me an appointment for a mammogram the next day.

"That can't be good," I thought. I went straight from the doctor's office to the movies, escaped into the second Harry Potter movie. I wanted to see the final performance Richard Harris gave before his death. I wanted not to think about the mammogram. I wanted to avoid the inevitable. I went to a twelve-step meeting, where I hoped to run into a woman I knew who had had breast cancer once and a recent scare. She told me the radiologist would give me an ultrasound after the mammogram and then probably conclude it was a benign cyst.

I steeled myself for the mammogram, which was painful. The X-ray tech went down the hall to consult with the radiologist and came back asking for more pictures, magnification views. Then she put the mammogram films up on the light box. I could see the lump. A bright white roundish lump with filaments radiating from it.

The conscious part of me that tells the truth whether or not the cognitive part of me wants to hear it was frankly horrified. "That is *not* nothing," I (she) thought.

Then the tech wanted to take me to ultrasound. I looked on the wall, where one of the printed flyers said radiologists follow mammogram with ultrasound when they suspect a benign cyst and thought: "Think cyst."

I had to interview someone for my column. She had been in a 1950s girl band, the one that recorded "My Boyfriend's Back" ("Hey na, hey na, my boyfriend's back"). I was still pretending I could go on with my normal life.

We scheduled the ultrasound for Thursday. I did the interview with the singer, went to Weight Watchers for a meeting, met my daughter for dinner at a Vietnamese restaurant, and took her to a movie.

Wednesday I went to my job, did another interview, and wrote a column. Thursday I went for my ultrasound, then back to work. Thursday afternoon the nurse practitioner who had done the breast exam called me.

At every stage of the diagnostic process I kept expecting someone to say to me, "It's nothing. Don't worry about it."

Only no one said that. Instead I kept being sent to the next scary appointment.

This time the nurse practitioner said she was sorry to call me at work with such bad news, but that the lump on my mammogram and ultrasound was "strongly suspicious." She referred me to a breast surgeon for an appointment for a needle biopsy the next day and told me about a breast cancer support group for recently diagnosed women.

I had to write another column, but I couldn't concentrate on my work, could barely put one sentence after another. I went to tell my editor, Mario, what was going on and why the column might not make much sense.

"I'm in the process of being diagnosed with breast cancer," I told him. Two women in our office had already had it.

"What do you mean 'in the process'?" he asked, and I explained the chain of events to him. "Well, it's Kaiser," he said. "They could be wrong."

He let me go home from work. I don't believe I've written another column since.

———————

I wasn't exactly sensible about my diagnosis. "If I have cancer,"
I thought, "I'll just die. I'll refuse treatment, take the palliative pain
medication, just die." This way of thinking came from a serious case
of hubris and an immense dose of faulty logic. I think I felt I would
welcome death, that it would be a relief. Or that I alone in the human race would deviate from the norm of wanting to do anything
possible to stay alive.

I've since learned that this is a luxury position. It can be held
with certainty only by someone who hasn't actually had to face the
diagnosis and the fear. It seems simple to make that decision, until
the fact of what it means is right in your face. *Treatment? No, thanks.
I'll take death.*

There are patients who do make that decision. And in light of
the blind panic that arises within you with the first pronouncement
of the words *breast cancer,* it can seem like a reasonable alternative at
first.

———————

The breast surgeon was a diminutive, pretty, tough-minded
Korean woman, new at Kaiser but a highly qualified specialist. She
told me what I already knew, that of course everyone suspected cancer. The tumor was what was called, in ironic misnomer, a healthy

size, almost three centimeters. The surgeon talked to me about possibilities and set me up for a fine-needle aspiration, drawing fluid from the tumor. When she returned from looking at the slides, she told me she was 99 percent sure it was breast cancer but wouldn't have the pathology report until the following Monday.

The previous Monday I had gone to the doctor with the peculiar skin. By Friday I'd been diagnosed with breast cancer.

Suddenly everything was different. Welcome to breast cancer land. Life as you know it is now over. All your plans, all your dreams have been replaced by nameless terrors and fears.

The surgeon and I discussed options. My right arm is severely impaired from when I broke my shoulder in 1991. I was afraid if lymph nodes were removed from under my arm, its functioning would be even further decreased. Above all, I didn't want to lose my ability to knit.

"If I can't knit and I can't write," I told the surgeon, "I won't have much quality of life. And I'm more concerned about quality of life than I am about preserving quantity at all costs."

"You won't do much knitting from the grave," she said. I had to take that under advisement.

I was terrified of chemotherapy, of the nausea, the debilitation, of having "chemo brain" and being unable to think clearly.

"What happens if I don't have surgery on the tumor?" I asked the surgeon.

"It will grow through the breast and ulcerate and smell really bad," she said. "You don't want that."

She was right. I didn't want that. From her office I went home to cry. For the next few days I wept, mourning for my lost plans and schemes. *First You Cry*, wrote Betty Rollins about her cancer diagnosis. But that's not the whole story. There are plenty of opportunities to cry. The information is so shocking, so frightening, so weighted with overtones of suffering and death that the only sane response you can have under the circumstances is to cry.

One by one, I told my family and friends. I put off telling my mother because she was eighty-two and had had a stroke during my previous cancer surgery. I didn't want to deal with her panic on top of my own.

I realized I would need the help of others and would also need to protect myself from their well-meaning questions, their sometimes intrusive expressions of care. It's not that I don't appreciate my friends—I do—but it takes energy I don't have to console them when I tell them I have cancer, to explain the treatments over and over, to socialize at times I can barely take care of myself.

For the past year or so, before the diagnosis, I had embraced solitude more than ever before. I often felt I had only a limited time left on earth to do what I needed to do. I resented people's wasting my time. Above all, I hated the telephone. When I am on the telephone, I can't knit, can't do needlepoint, can't write.

In order to write, I need long stretches of uninterrupted time. I need to be alone with my thoughts. I need to sink down into the sometimes crazy realm of the wild unconscious from which my writ-

ing springs. Heaven to me is a wide-open day with nothing scheduled, a day to take a long walk by myself and come home to write
or to knit.

I love my family and friends. I know I am fortunate to have
them in my life. Love is immensely important to me. But for some
reason I feel a terrible urgency to complete the work that is mine.
The older I get, the more life seems to be about the work.

"Time is what we have not got enough of," Hemingway is reputed to have said.

Finally I accepted that I needed to have surgery and tried not
to look too far ahead. One thing I've learned in twelve-step recovery
has really served me well: Just do the next right thing. All you have
to do today is today. Tomorrow will take care of itself. Just take care
of the next twenty-four hours.

───────

My grandmother Mama Yetta used to say, "If you have your
health, you have everything." For the six months or so before my
breast cancer diagnosis, my health had been going to hell. I went
through several months of shortness of breath, which no one could
diagnose or treat properly and which left me so frantic with worry
that one night I wrote out my last will and testament and left it on
my kitchen table in case I died in my sleep.

Then, in November, I had had such severe abdominal pains
during the night that early in the morning I called 911 and went to

the emergency room. That was diagnosed as an intestinal obstruction, thought to have been caused by adhesions from a previous surgery eight years before.

I believe now that my body was trying to get my attention.

At the end of my father's life, the last few times he landed up in intensive care there was so much wrong with him that doctors could not fix one problem without making another one worse.

In middle age, it seems, everything that happens turns out to be a chronic problem you have to learn how to manage. My right arm, which had been broken eleven years before, was in bad shape. I had become accustomed to a fair amount of pain. Much of the surgery done for breast cancer, in which the axillary or underarm lymph nodes are removed, would further damage my arm.

I worried about not being able to knit. Was I addicted to knitting, or was it merely a passion so important to me that I didn't care to live without it?

I feared my life's being consumed by breast cancer as much as I feared the treatments. I began to think of my life before breast cancer as having been an innocent or halcyon time, though of course I'd been sure I was suffering mightily with emotional or job-related pain.

On the advice of my nurse practitioner, I joined a breast cancer support group at Kaiser. My first night there I knitted in the waiting room. I was nervous about everything—my diagnosis, coming to the group for the first time, becoming involved with a whole new group of people—and I knitted to keep my anxiety at bay. I was working on a lace scarf of ultrafine merino wool hand-painted in shades of pumpkin and moss green. It was in my favorite lace pattern, feather and fan.

I knitted inside the group too. I thought the cofacilitators would ask me to stop, but they didn't. I felt that my knitting was keeping the other participants at arm's length and that they felt as uncomfortable with me, the newest member, as I did with them. As the group wore on, however, and we became more animated and at ease, they began to ask me about my knitting.

"Oh, you got here just in time," one of the women said. "We were just saying we wanted to add knitting to this group."

———

I had good doctors, but I had to come up with my own sorts of healing potions too. For me, one way or another, those potions must always contain a large dose of needles and yarn or needles and thread. So I undertook to treat myself oncologically with the healing power of craft.

I was surprised to find during this time that needlepoint began to take the place of knitting in my life. When I awoke at four in the morning in stark terror and dread, I still took refuge in needlework, but now I stitched tapestry instead of knitting.

I had a Kaffe Fassett canvas titled "Autumn Roses" that a friend (also a cancer survivor) had given me. Typical of Fassett's work, it featured painterly use of color and shading. I worked on this picture obsessively, in the dead of night, or whenever I couldn't bear to talk, read, or hear any more about breast cancer.

Kaffe Fassett, the renowned designer, was raised in Big Sur, where his parents owned Nepenthe. Though primarily a painter, and now based in London, he has become known for designing fiber art that employs exuberant use of color and complex combinations of pattern. His sister Holly, who also knits, still owns Nepenthe, a café and store. Nepenthe has some of the best views on the entire California coast, which is really saying something. I always think of Kaffe growing up as a child amid all that beauty.

The needlepoint I did had five large roses in red, yellow, pink, and white. Each was shaded in many colors. The alternations of coral, blue-green, lemon yellow, dark green, burgundy, and shades of shocking pink filled my senses and calmed my mind. I stitched until I was tired and could sleep. I have no idea why that particular needlepoint so appealed to me in that moment of life's calamities or why it did so much to alleviate the panic. It was probably a result Kaffe Fassett never had in mind when designing, but it worked out that way anyhow.

The needlepoint was quiet, repetitive work. Yet it had a transformative quality. For each stitch of needlepoint, you have to look at the tiniest detail, separating each dot of color from the ones beside it, focusing only on that one point, which becomes, in T. S. Eliot's phrase, "the still point of the turning world." So you do one and then another. When that section of the canvas is completed, it becomes nearly invisible. It has been subsumed into the whole so thoroughly that the detail you've just been working has disappeared from view.

The same thing happens in knitting. You focus on the work at hand, the stitch, the row, the color, the pattern. You operate within the tiniest fragment of detail. Yet once it is completed, you will never see that section of work in the same way again. It disappears into the whole. That's why it is futile to worry overly much about mistakes. Most of them end up invisible anyway.

I like what Norman Kennedy has to say about mistakes. When you point out to him a glaring error that has inadvertently occurred in a piece of complex knitting, he will reply, "Aye, but would a man running for his life notice it?"

———

Unable to sleep, I would open my bag of yarns and begin applying color to the canvas in arrangements of tiny dots, like a pointillist painter. One dot after another, one color after another, one rose after another, one leaf after another, until I could fall back asleep. Sometimes I would look up to see the world transformed by my needlepoint. Instead of a solid swath of orange in a sunset, I would notice the yellows and reds and violets inside the color, the infiltrations of lighter and darker blue.

I have found needlepoint, like knitting, to be soothing, compelling, and addictive. You always want to see how the next color is going to look and how it will change the look of the whole. Just one more color, we say to ourselves, as in knitting we say, just one more row. And so we keep going, row by row, color by color, stitch by stitch, until the project is suddenly complete.

I think about my father a lot as I confront my own mortality. Breast cancer is my second bout with cancer. The first time I believed that you had it, took care of it, and went on with your life, changed in some way, a cancer survivor, but not a walking time bomb.

Now I think that once you have had cancer you are always at risk for having another cancer.

My first was renal cell carcinoma.

"That's a peculiar cancer," my gastroenterologist told me on the phone recently. "We don't really know what it will do."

I like my gastroenterologist. She is a plainspoken woman. "Let's face it," she once told me. "Half of us will die from cancer, and the other half from heart disease."

She went on to tell me that renal cell carcinoma was sometimes associated with tumors of the retina or brain.

"We used to tell people with kidney or, yes, breast cancer, that after three years they were out of the woods. Then we changed it to five, then ten, then twenty. Now we don't say anything."

The implications were clear and also conversant with what I was beginning to believe myself. In the breast cancer support group I belonged to, some women took the approach that they would go all out to fight the cancer, eliminate it from their bodies, and then go on with their lives.

Because it was my second time, I couldn't quite believe that.

As it turns out, this disquieting open-endedness is an integral part of the breast cancer experience. Once you've had it, it is never quite far from your consciousness or out of your life. Hard as it may be to face, you are never really out of the woods.

"How do you know when you're cured of breast cancer?" goes a black humor joke.

"When you die of something else," is the not-so-funny answer.

12. The Waiting Is the Hardest Part

UNTIL THE OFFICIAL DELIVERY OF THE PATHOLOGY RE-
port, whose contents would decide my future for
months to come, I was in a holding pattern.

Finally, the surgeon told me she had good news
and bad news. The good news was that the margins
were clean and the lymph nodes showed no signs
of cancer. The bad news was that the nucleus of the
tumor was high-grade, meaning the cancer was aggressive. It made it more likely, she said, that the oncologist would recommend chemotherapy.

In shock from the diagnosis and recovering
from the surgery, I felt fragile, vulnerable, emotionally
flayed. I experienced a newfound sympathy and compassion for women who have gone through this in the

past and will have to go through it in the future, the sisterhood of the breast cancer veterans.

For some reason, this cancer affected my emotions far more than the renal cell carcinoma had. The breast is more delicate, female, connected to how we nourish others and are ourselves nurtured.

I could say from my experience of kidney cancer that once you begin losing body parts, you are not exactly anxious to relinquish more. Perhaps someone who hadn't already lost a kidney and much of the use of her right arm might have been more sanguine about having a mastectomy and being done with it, but I sought to keep what tissue I could.

I began to think about my relationships. Had I nurtured the wrong people? This seemed fairly obvious. How had I been nurtured myself? As a culture, our relationship to Mother Earth and the great feminine principle is in a bad way. Many of us are disconnected from the web of community and networks of villages and extended families that sustained us in the not-so-distant past. One woman in our support group said that after her diagnosis she had felt "cut from the herd." Another said that she had felt completely untethered to anything, as if she were floating in space.

Her image reminded me of how I'd felt when Billy left me for the other woman. I'd felt unmoored, drifting. It seems ludicrous now that I could have imagined such an unreliable creature would hold me fast to earth, but imagine it I had. I thought our joining would make me normal, whole in the Platonic sense of the word, like two halves of the same entity finding each other and recombining to become one.

————

The diagnosis of breast cancer made me feel earthbound, tied to a physical body that promised to subject me to a great deal of discomfort.

I was accustomed to having a lot of energy and to pushing myself to do more. My job involved a lot of work, and I drove myself to walk, shop for groceries, knit, write, and go to meetings besides. Twelve- to fourteen-hour days were my norm. Now, on medical leave from my job, I needed a nap in the afternoon and was afraid I would become too tired to do anything at all.

On the positive side, I was forced to take care of myself. I had to put myself first, judge which situations and people sustained me and which drained my energy, decide whom I wanted to see and what I wanted to do, search within myself for whatever meaning and benefit could be contained within this illness.

I struggled for acceptance. The cancer was here, and I had to deal with it. There was no way I could minimize it or make it go away.

————

Now I do the needlepoint in total silence, no TV, no music, with the phone unplugged much of the time. More than knitting, needlepoint is grounded in the present. Blue here, white there, just keep going. The thread twirls around over the needle and comes to rest on the canvas in a pleasing circular shape. The finished result looks beaded, and I have always loved beadwork. At times I have imagined that the spirit world looks as though it were constructed of tiny glass beads.

In needlepoint, as in beadwork or yarn painting, you create the world. One day I was making water. Each tiny stitch of blue, white, gray, or pearlized white contributed to the depiction of a vast expanse of water. In that minuscule way, I might have been imitating the Creator, making the world a detail at a time: the oceans, the mountains, the clear blue sky. Each discrete bump of color helps contribute to the whole, and as the focus is so pointedly narrow, I don't think too far ahead. Each arrangement of stitches is also immensely satisfying, transforming the canvas from an empty grid to a colorful scene.

There is more creativity in knitting, more decisions to be made about fit and shaping and mathematics. Needlepoint is simpler. It frees the creative part of my brain to write. It calms me in the dead of night, like meditation in luminous blackness that returns to me the perspective of eternity.

At a twelve-step meeting recently, I heard the speaker say that in sobriety she had developed "a life of quiet fulfillment." I could relate to that because my routine of solitude, knitting, writing, and needlepoint provided me with a life of quiet fulfillment.

I was working on a picture of two striped fish swimming in a tropical sea. I needed to go to Stitchbirds, the big needlepoint store in Marin County. The owner of the store talked me into metallic thread, much to my daughter's dismay.

"You're turning into Nanny," my daughter said, alluding to my mother's well-known love of bright colors and shiny textures.

I had thought the fish would appeal to my daughter, Shuna, who has taken the word *Fish* as her middle name and nom de plume. But the iridescent thread put her right off the entire project.

————

Partly I bought the underwater scene of two fish because it reminded me of the fish tanks at Kaiser, where I receive my medical care. Kaiser Permanente, headquartered in Oakland, may well have been the nation's first HMO. Henry Kaiser started it to provide medical care to the workers in his shipyards, who poured into Oakland and Richmond in the early 1940s, during the war, from rural outposts in Texas and Louisiana.

Those migrations turned Oakland into a city with an influential black population. Descendants of those shipworkers receive their medical care at Kaiser today. The medical facility is so vast that I've taken to calling it the City of Kaiser, and since my breast cancer diagnosis I've been spending quite a bit of time there.

In both the surgery and radiology waiting rooms, there are large saltwater fish tanks. Perhaps there is research to the effect that looking at moving fish calms patients down, particularly patients in dire straits as the surgery and X-ray patients tend to be.

In the tank in the surgery waiting room, there is a large lionfish with red and white striped waving tentacles. My favorite, how-ever, is a far stranger-looking creature. Its scales are pointed at the end like fish bones rather than pearlescent paillettes, in a two-toned pattern. Its eyes are a striking metallic blue, with flecks in it like the metallic paint of a customized car.

I was thinking of those metallic blue eyes as I purchased the metallic thread, almost against my will.

"That metallic thread looks good in underwater scenes," said the shop owner. "It will make your picture pretty."

I used it to make a big puddle, which too late I realized was supposed to be coral rather than water. Oh, well. Better to contem-plate striped fish and metallic thread than the immediate threat of chemotherapy or radiation.

So I travel this journey through cancer one step after another, fashioning one stitch at a time in a picture that may never have any earthly use to anyone at all. It reminds me of the joy I felt in color-ing when I was very small. It takes my mind off my problems and calms my emotions. It pleases my eyes and soothes my spirit. I sup-pose that ought to be reason enough to do it.

Today I am making branch coral.

———

In general, I have a hard time wrapping my mind around the fact that my life may be in danger. As my friend Iris once asked me, "Is this serenity or is it denial?" I just can't tell.

Because of the size of my tumor, the aggressive nature of its

DNA, and the presence of the HER2neu oncogene, Dr. Gordon, my medical oncologist, recommended chemo, my biggest fear.

This set off a storm of indecision in me. On one side, I think, "My tumor was aggressive, and I should attack the possibility of any remaining cancer aggressively." On the other side, I think, "My immune system is already compromised, and the risks from chemotherapy don't seem worth the possible benefits."

The oncologists proposed to eliminate the possibility of microscopic rogue cancer cells that might or might not be roaming my body. They recommended a toxic regimen of drugs that would destroy, albeit temporarily, my immune system. Possible risks include heart damage, leukemia, mental confusion, and skin ulceration if the chemicals leak out of the vein.

When I told Dr. Gordon that I am writing a book and am concerned about how the chemo will affect my thinking, he said, "Forget the book. Just take care of this right now."

He was probably right, but at the time it sounded like the opposite of treating the whole person.

———

Sometime during the torturous decision-making time, I felt my spirit rise up inside me as a tangible thing. The only experience I could connect it to was one I had when my daughter was a baby and I was breast-feeding her. When I took her to the pediatrician, he said she wasn't gaining weight fast enough, meaning she wasn't getting enough nutrition, and I would have to stop nursing her.

My daughter was a happy, contented baby. She was thriving and peaceful and nursed like a dream.

I felt something come alive in me at that moment. I became like a mother tiger defending her cubs from danger. I picked up my baby, walked out of that office, and never went back. I didn't regret my decision for a second.

In *Women Who Run with the Wolves*, Clarissa Pinkola Estes writes about that instinctive, knowing animal part of woman that has been lost in our technological universe. I've met her before in myself, the soft animal part, the fierce defender of the family, the ferocious protector of life.

Being a knitter, I've spent a lot of time in my own company. My hands have connected me to an ancient heritage. The image of a woman holding a needle and thread seems almost like an archetypal symbol to me now. She's Penelope waiting for Ulysses to return, Demeter following her daughter Persephone into the underworld, Ariadne escaping from the labyrinth of the Minotaur by following a single, silken thread.

She's the fabled wild woman, and she's fought the paternalistic medical establishment before.

During my pregnancy with my daughter, I told the obstetrician I wanted natural childbirth and asked if he did it. "Oh, yes," he answered. "I do it all the time."

I attended Lamaze classes and prepared for the birth. After my daughter had been delivered, the obstetrician said to me. "That's the first natural childbirth delivery I've ever done."

"I thought you said you did them all the time," I said.

"Oh," he said, "all women say they want natural childbirth, but no one wants to go through with it once the pain starts."

Not long afterward I reviewed a book about birth for *Ms.* magazine. The book, *Birth Without Violence*, was by Dr. Frederick Leboyer, who advocated giving birth in warm-water tanks, in semidarkness, placing the baby curled up on the mother's stomach, and not cutting the umbilical cord until the cord stopped beating.

Dr. Leboyer claimed that bringing a baby into the world in harsh light with loud noises, snapping its curled spine straight, smacking it on the behind during its first moments, and making it breathe without the umbilical cord before it was ready were the source of many of our spinal and psychological problems.

"When you have a baby in an American hospital," I wrote in my article, "you understand why we're in Vietnam."

Nowadays I make that connection between the way our society views women and nurturing and the way it views the earth. As the earth goes, so go we. Her nurturing functions have been defiled, contaminated, dismissed with contempt. And we women, as one of her intimate by-products, have an epidemic of cancer in the most nurturing parts of our body, our breasts.

So we are poisoned and contaminated from the toxins we put in our air, water, and soil, which cause us to develop cancer, and then the cancer is treated by cutting, burning, and poisoning. What's wrong with this picture?

Before deciding about chemotherapy, I went to have a CT scan of my abdominal area to make sure it was clear of cancer. When the CT scan was over, my daughter was waiting for me. We had arranged to meet for a meal. Over food, I told her I was leaning toward refusing chemotherapy. I told her about medical experiences I'd had with her birth and breast-feeding. I told her how I had dug in my heels for ten years, refusing hormone replacement therapy despite my doctors' entreaties and how time had proved me right.

"I've always had love and respect for you, and it's only gotten bigger through all these things," my daughter said. Both of us cried and held each other. This was a scary time for both of us, me for my health, her for her mom.

I had been reading *Refuge* by Terry Tempest Williams. She writes about how at thirty-four she became the matriarch of her large Mormon family after her mother, grandmothers, and other female relatives had succumbed to cancer. She talked about the tribe of one-breasted women to which she belonged.

She describes the atomic tests that were performed in Nevada and Utah during the 1950s. She saw an actual mushroom cloud early one morning as her family drove through the desert. She talks about how the federal government described the Utah desert where her family lives, and which holds the Great Salt Lake and a vast bird refuge dear to her heart, as a virtually uninhabited place.

She made the connection between the condition of the earth and the condition of her female relatives.

To be fair to the medical community, it has come a long way toward treating breast cancer, ensuring longer survival times and better care. Breast cancer is no longer the death sentence it once was. But it is a symptom of a much larger problem. And the deeper problem needs prevention, rather than cure.

How do we care for ourselves? For one another? For the earth that is our mother and our only home? How do we care for our damaged bodies, our fragile souls?

Do we slash, poison, and burn to repair the damage that's been done before, buying time until the cutting and burning cause secondary problems? Do we go deep inside, searching for the source of the pain, rooting it out, addressing it spiritually, from the depths of the heart and the quiet knowing of the soul? Or do we do both, hoping something, anything will work?

It's not so much whether I live or die that's important to me; it's the way I live or die. It's the way I honor my deepest self, my knowing, my animal female part, the wild woman of the forest, who once knew her way around animals, plants, and herbs, the one who could talk to birds in their own language.

The wild woman is the one who knits, the one who is comforted by the quiet rhythms of stitching and craft. I think I've trusted her before to good effect, and I'm going to have to trust her again.

———

I make my decision and then have to change it. Dr. Gordon, my Kaiser oncologist, recommends chemo. With radiation, he says, I have a 60 percent chance of survival. Tamoxifen adds another 10 to

15 percent. Then chemo adds another 10 percent to that. Ironically, having the HER2neu oncogene increases the possibility of success with chemo, making the tumor cells more responsive.

When I press him, he says that 50 percent of the women doctors treat to prevent recurrence are already cured. "We just don't know which fifty percent," he says.

Of course I don't want chemo. I will do everything in my power to avoid chemo. I am planning to refuse chemo.

"Because of the size of your tumor, they will recommend chemo," says Leonne, a friend from L.A. who's an oncology nurse. "Definitely."

Dr. Veronica Shim, my surgeon, talks to an oncologist at UCSF. She says he recommends chemo too. I do my best to separate Veronica from the Kaiser oncology establishment, to get the most independent opinion she can give me. I offer her confidentiality. She still recommends chemo.

"That's pretty good," Lou says, "for her to hold her ground with you when you're trying hard to get your way. Not many people could do that."

I go with my friend Marilyn for my second opinion at UCSF with Dr. Pamela Klein. She works there half-time; the other half she works at Genentech, doing research connected to the HER2neu gene.

"It is the nature of breast cancer to spread," she says. "Once it spreads, we can't cure it. We can cure it only at this stage."

It's entirely possible that the surgery has already gotten all the cancer, but what if it hasn't? Do I really want metastases to my bones, my lungs, my liver?

"No responsible person would tell you to refuse chemo," says David Bloom, my sister and brother-in-law's doctor friend in Florida. "This isn't Iraq we're talking about here. It's Japan and Nazi Germany. You have to fight with the biggest army and toughest guns you have. No one who has been in the trenches, who has taken care of people who are really sick with cancer, would advise you to give up this one chance for a cure."

All right. I've heard enough. I've thought enough. I'm mentally exhausted. All I think about is chemo or not chemo. I go to doctors' appointments. I talk to professionals. I talk to women who've been there in the past, who are going through it now, who are just a little bit ahead of me. The decision consumes all my time, all my energy.

Little by little I'm watching my immediate future slip away. Writing my book. My planned two weeks as a writer-in-residence at the Ucross Foundation in Wyoming. Any possibility of a normal life for the next ten months, year, two years, five years. It is a staggering prospect. I suppose I should be grateful that I didn't realize what this would involve right off the bat and that I have any chance at all for survival. But what could I have done? I have no choice but to deal with it.

"I'm taking a long time to make this decision," I tell Dr. Gordon.

"I would too," he says. "But I told you before, if it were me, I would do it."

I'm too young to have already had two cancers, says David Bloom. I have a good chance for a cure, says Pamela Klein. I'm too young to die, says Veronica Shim.

———

My friend Melanie Lewis, a fellow knitter, is a little ahead of me in the breast cancer protocol. She is approaching her third chemo treatment as I am trying to make up my mind whether to begin the first.

"You're in the worst part," Melanie says. "Once you start treatment, it gets easier."

"I don't know what's happened to me," I tell her. "I'm hardly knitting. My desire to knit anything new has flown away."

Melanie says she's been knitting the same lace scarf over and over. "Anything with shaping is beyond me," she says.

Come to think of it, that's what I'm doing too. Knitting the same lace scarf (though not the same as Melanie's) again and again. I'm currently on my fourth one. Sweaters, with their calculations and decisions, seem out of my reach. Perhaps I've ceased to believe in a future in which to wear them. Perhaps I'm just mentally exhausted. Breast cancer has eaten my brain.

I'm surprised to find this, because if anything, I thought knitting would sustain me in such a crisis. It was so therapeutic during my father's decline and death that it could have been prescribed as a medicine in itself. Not anymore. I work on my lace scarf in the various waiting rooms that have come to define my life, but my heart isn't in it. I have enthusiasm only for needlepoint, which I now do when I wake up, first thing in the morning.

Currently I'm working my way through a Kaffe Fassett series of small floral studies. They are exceedingly simple and as repetitious as my lace scarves. But the rhythm of the stitches, the tiny pinpoint focus of each stitch, each color, each filled-in space, comforts and consoles me.

I find after a certain amount of time doing needlepoint I am in a different frame of mind. It's not like the alpha state achieved by the rhythms of knitting, which feels more like a free fall into possibilities and creativity. This is more of a tranquil state, a break from anxiety, concentration on an activity so simple that it requires nothing more than a steady hand and a good source of light.

———

I make my first appointment for chemo. I have things to do to get ready. I'm trying to get my house in order so that someone could possibly come over and help take care of me. I am assembling the essentials I will need to have around me, groceries, vitamins, nutritional supplements, books.

I imagine a white sterile room. I can picture myself enduring chemo if I can be in such a room. Whether or not it is imaginary is immaterial, just so long as it is pure and white.

But first I have something else I want to do. The Stitches Market, a huge knitters' convention, is coming to downtown Oakland at the end of February. I've been looking forward to it all year, ever since the last one. Stitches is an overwhelming, exhilarating, inspiring riot of color and yarn, patterns and buttons, numberless knitters in their handmade creations. I want to go there before I do anything else. There are people there I want to connect with. I'm hoping it will reignite my interest in knitting.

So I schedule my first chemo appointment for the week after Stitches. I'm resigned to postponing my writer's residency. I accept the necessity of filling the next year or two with unpleasant lifesaving treatments. I'm barely knitting at the moment. But I can't give up the possibility for inspiration.

Perhaps this is a process that proceeds in stages, like the stages of grief. In its own way, it is a cousin to grief and loss. Diagnosis. Denial. Decision. Acceptance. Treatment. Recovery. And the big if, cure.

13. The Sisters
of Knitting

THE FIRST YEAR I WENT TO STITCHES, IN 1997, WHEN I
signed books in one of the booths, I thought my head
was going to explode. There were hundreds of busy,
bustling knitters, wearing their plenitude of handknit
sweaters as they browsed among the vendors of yarn,
buttons, patterns, paraphernalia. The booths were
filled with thousands of balls of dazzling yarns, each
color more luscious, each texture more touchable,
than the next. Bright lights, big city, it was like going
to a carnival. I suffered from sensory overload and developed a massive headache.

Then I learned the trick of how to do it. That
was to go on Friday, when the convention was more
sparsely attended, look around, and get my bearings.
When it comes to buying yarn, I am extremely poky

about making up my mind. It can take me years of thinking to decide whether or not to buy a certain yarn. I had to give myself extra time at the crowded marketplace. I could return the next day, Saturday, and buy what I wanted. That way I had a chance to assimilate what I had seen, consider what I wanted to own, process all the sensory input.

It was an overwhelming experience to be among hundreds of people who were similarly impassioned to do what I most often did alone. It was fascinating to see knitted creations, worn by real people, in living color. Every two-dimensional paper pattern, every design from a knitting magazine of the past year, every Fair Isle kit you'd seen advertised, every picture of a project that had fired your imagination, all came alive and paraded around the room.

Since Stitches took place at the convention center in downtown Oakland, I wrote several newspaper columns about it. The first one mainly concerned the wild and unconventional knitting designer Lily Chin and the book she was writing about hip young urban knitters, a group she called HYUKs.

The second was about a group called Bikers Who Knit. This was a joke my Rolfer, Michael Salveson, and I dreamed up. We had been talking about how knitting suffered from image problems and needed a public relations overhaul. The group we came up with, Knitting Terrorists, lost its humor after September 11, 2001, so we decided to go with Bikers Who Knit.

Bikers Who Knit was a motorcycle gang. The members would have tattoos on their arms reading "Born to Raise Yarn." Their "colors" would sport a ball of yarn with two needles crossing through it. They would have nicknames such as Fair Isle Frank and Cable Charlie. They would come roaring into downtown Oakland on their vroom-vroom Harleys to shop at the Stitches marketplace, and the giant convention center would fall silent with a frisson of fear.

Actually, the concept of combining knitting with political subversion was not far off the mark. A Canadian man named Grant Neufeld has used a ball of yarn with a lit fuse as the logo for his organization, Revolutionary Knitting Circle.

I wrote a humor column about Bikers Who Knit. While I was researching it by strolling around the Oakland Convention Center, Cheryl Oberle, the hand dyer and knitting designer, whom I had met at the previous year's Stitches, told me she sometimes knitted sitting on the back of her husband's Harley, drawing astonished stares from other drivers on the road. She also said that Elizabeth Zimmermann, the übermama of modern American knitting, had also married a motorcyclist and was known to do the same.

Cheryl told me an urban legend. A couple went camping in a remote campground somewhere in the boonies. The husband went off to fish, leaving his wife in the camp, where she planned to work on her knitting. She was working on some mittens. She had been sitting quietly for some time when she heard the loud roar of unmuffled engines, and a pair of bikers on Harleys pulled into the camp. She was all alone and felt frightened.

"What are you knitting there?" asked one of the bikers.

"Mittens," answered the knitter.

"I'd put some color in those if I were you," the biker said. "Those are the kinds of mittens that get left at the side of the road."

Then, as the story goes, the biker lifted up his pants leg to show off a pair of extravagantly colored, knitted-by-hand socks. After that biker and knitter chatted happily about gauge, color, and pattern repeats.

Cheryl was one of the friends I made at Stitches. By the time I met her, I had knitted several patterns from her book, *Folk Shawls*, and I found her to be as warm and simpatico as the stories that accompanied each shawl.

We e-mailed back and forth and made plans to meet in 2003. Stitches is a place where everyone who has written a knitting book comes, to teach classes or simply to network with other knitters.

I went to see Cheryl at her booth. She told me she had been in a devastating car crash a few months before and had been slowly recovering.

Cheryl lives in Denver and leads retreats called Knitaways at various places in the western United States. She was at one of these retreats, in some snowy mountains, when her pickup truck was broadsided by a speeding ambulance.

"I heard a whoosh," she told me. "Then everything went white. It was like I was enfolded by wings, in white water that was almost particulate. I could hear a conversation going on in the distance. The people who saw me in the truck thought I was dead, that my neck had been broken. Then I thought, 'Where are the colors?' and suddenly I was back in my body."

She is a soft person, but she seemed more fragile, more on the verge of tears, than I had seen her before. I told her I was dealing with breast cancer and was soon to start chemotherapy.

We met in a group of eight knitters for dinner. Everyone was an author of books, teacher of techniques, or vendor of her own designs and brands of yarns.

"I believe I'm the worst knitter here," I said to the group, surveying the heavy hitters gathered at the table. "I'm almost never in that situation."

Being knitting ladies, we got right to the point.

"Breast cancer totally transformed me," said Joyce Williams, who has written a book about Latvian knitting. "Before I got breast cancer, I had been knitting for forty years as a blind follower."

"Can you imagine Joycie as a blind follower?" asked Lizzie Upitis, who wrote a book about Latvian mittens and now works at one of the Deepak Chopra centers.

"If the pattern said, 'Cross left,' I crossed left," continued Joyce. "If the pattern said, 'Cross right,' I crossed right. But after my mastectomy I decided to go to knitting camp. I met Elizabeth Zimmermann, and she changed my life. She was watching me knit one day, and she said, 'You know, you're not supposed to look at the book. You're supposed to look at your knitting.' I had never understood the principles of anything I was knitting."

Cheryl talked some more about her accident and the "angel" who had shown up on the scene to help her, a person unknown to her who had made sure her purse went in the ambulance with her, contacted her Knitaway group and her husband to tell them where she was, visited her in the emergency room, advocated for her, and helped calm her fears.

After my dinner with the knitting ladies, I felt as if I had been encircled by a group of nurturing females who protected and supported me. Something was being born in me from my ordeal with breast cancer, and the women in my life would enfold me while I was in the vulnerable position of giving birth to it.

What all the women had spoken about in their knitting was the process of becoming more completely themselves. I was on disability at that time, temporarily freed from the demands of my newspaper column. I found myself drawn back more and more into the knitting world I loved. I helped Linda Borof teach classes at the Knitting Basket, did readings from *The Knitting Sutra*, pursued friendships with other knitters.

Survivors of breast cancer are extraordinarily generous in their willingness to help other women through the labyrinth of choices and perils. My main breast cancer buddy, Melanie, had had surgery a few months before I did. Because she was a knitter, and a cancer survivor, she always went straight to the heart of the matter. I could tell her almost anything that was bothering me and hear some useful wisdom back. I also called friends of friends for advice and appealed to the women in my support group for a way through the woods.

I ran into Melanie at Stitches with Laura, a young woman we know, whose entire personality and sense of being have been transformed by learning to knit. She is a dedicated knitter and quiet inside. She makes pieces of lace out of interesting material and frames them stretched out in shadow boxes. The last time I saw her, she was knitting lace from a blend of stainless steel and silk, marketed by the Japanese house of yarn, Habu.

Habu stopped traffic last year at Stitches. The lines to get into its booth were so long that they clogged the aisles. Habu sells yarns made of paper, of soy fiber, of bamboo, made by the same process used to extract rayon from tree pulp.

I have attended Stitches only on the West Coast. There are expos in the East and the Midwest as well. According to public radio's *Marketplace* show, thirty-eight million women in America knit. Of those, four million started in 2003. The percentage of women under forty-five who knit has doubled from 9 to 18. Stitches was so well attended in 2004 that it has outgrown its convention space and will not be held in Oakland next year.

When I began knitting seriously again in 1991, the world of handknitting resembled a somewhat moribund cult of older practitioners whose skills were in danger of vanishing from the earth. When I moved back to the East Bay in 1988, there were six yarn stores in my region. Several years later there were two. Though it has always had its diehard adherents, knitting was so unpopular and déclassé, as recently as 1996, that my book editor advised me not to put the word *knitting* in the title lest I sacrifice sales.

Younger knitting enthusiasts are now transforming the somewhat hokey province of handknitting from the frumpy to the hip.

They are demanding and getting patterns for more up-to-date styles, inspiring the imaginations of novelty yarn designers, expanding again the business of selling yarn. The yarn stores in my area now number six again, most opened within the past two years.

In addition to sweaters and socks, young knitters now create pillows, wristlets, felted purses, tea cozies, art pieces, flowers, and whimsical scarves by the mile. I was with my daughter recently at Article Pract (the name is a Spoonerism on *practical art*), a yarn store in Oakland, when she took me to look at something in the window. It was a knitted amaryllis in its three stages of being: spike, bud, and fully opened flower. Everything, including the pots and squiggles of fake moss on top of the dirt, had been knitted of yarn.

That's not the kind of knitting I want to do, but that doesn't mean I can't appreciate its originality and brilliance, the skill that it takes to conceive and execute such a thing.

During my bout with breast cancer, I went to Stitches because I wanted to become reinspired to knit. Everything new in the world of knitting was previewed there or at the wholesale trade shows. Last year I found hand-painted cashmere from Mongolia at a reasonable price and buttons made of handblown glass.

For months I had been consumed by the intense mental and physical process of diagnosis and surgery. At Stitches, I felt my desire to knit rekindle, though it was still some time before I actively began stitching again.

My encounters with the knitting ladies were close to spiritual experiences. Our conversations were deep and profound. It has occurred to me more than once that knitting owes much of its power to the strength of female friendship. One time a friend observed me knitting and said, "They shouldn't say you need a lot of patience to knit. They should say you need a lot of spirit."

The knitting ladies were only one of the sisterhoods that saw me through this time. My women's group of Arica meditators gathered around me and boosted me on waves of love, energizing me for each phase of treatment. My women friends from the old days in Berkeley, from Judith's circle of Buddhist and poet friends, from the Floating Lotus Magic Opera commune, the copy desk at ANG Newspapers, the *Oakland Tribune* newsroom, the women's movement, my sisters and cousins and daughter and mother, the women I knew in twelve-step programs, my literary agent and book editor, all offered help, support, rides, supper, a shoulder to cry on, a person to care.

Not to shortchange my male friends either, because they showed up to help in solid numbers.

Much of the healing energy I needed, however, had to be summoned from deep inside myself. It came while I knitted, or wrote, or patiently added stitches to a needlepoint canvas. The spirit I needed to feel rise up within me had to be provided by the intentional practice of craft. It may have been a solitary pursuit, but it connected me to generations of women who had toiled in the same vineyards, producing the same arts. The healing power of craft is tied up with communities. Think of quilting circles, lacemakers, the shawl-knitting women in Orenburg, Russia, who sell their work through a collective organization.

Groups of women have probably gathered to do needlework together since the dawn of time. When our fingers are busy, our minds are free to expand, and conversation flows swift and deep.

I treasure time with the sisterhood of knitters. They validate and affirm me, share my sufferings or confide their own, unite in pursuit of a strangely solitary yet social activity that both deepens and is deepened by the power of female fellowship.

If a force like this could ever be collected—who knows?—it could rule the world.

14. Accepting the Inevitable

I TALK ON THE PHONE TO BETTINA, THE SISTER OF JUDITH, my friend who committed suicide last November, about four months ago. We talk about grief. Bettina says she can hardly bear to look at anything from Italy. She goes to a Tuscan restaurant and has to run outside to the street to cry. Judith went to Italy every summer for years. I believe Bettina joined her on many of these trips. It's said that Judith wanted her ashes divided among Berkeley, Florence, and Venice.

For the past year and a half I've grieved hard for my father. In my mind the breast cancer is all tied up with grief. Like prolonged depression, grief suppresses your immune system. I worry about Bettina and Ray, Judith's husband of thirty-five years.

Grief is unavoidable, mourning appropriate.

When does it turn to morbidity, like the endless mourning of the Victorians, following the example of their queen, Victoria, who elevated grief for her husband, Prince Albert, to an art form? How can you grieve without causing irreparable harm to your body? How much grief was stored in my tumor? Did it vanish with the surgery? Or did the diagnosis and surgery create another well of grief in the same place?

The first time I had a biopsy of a lump in my right breast was in 1973. I had just turned thirty. I was in a relationship with a man who I had believed would finally satisfy my unfilled need to be loved the way I wanted, to be cherished and valued as I hadn't been by my father, to be rescued by the great savior of romantic love.

My disappointment over the failure of that relationship contributed, I believe, to the fibroid cyst that formed in my breast, a cyst that had been started, I also believe, by hormone shots given to me in London to stop my milk after I delivered my stillborn baby.

Bettina talked about her grief over Judith's being all mixed up with grief for her mother. "Even though my mother had Alzheimer's and hadn't spoken for years, some part of me still believed she would become the mother I had always wanted," she said. "I was devastated when she died because that hope was gone."

My experience with grief is that any fresh grief builds a pipeline to all the grief that's gone before. The past grief, the stored grief, the bottomless well and pit of grief all rise to the surface together. Certainly by middle age, much of what we deal with emotionally is loss: disappointment, death, and loss. Serious loss wakes you up. It forces you to pay attention. You can't come through it unchanged and unscathed. And it happens to everyone.

———————

In *Sacred Clowns,* one of Tony Hillerman's mysteries set on the Navajo reservation, Jim Chee, a tribal policeman, attempts to describe *hozho*, the Navajo word for harmony, to someone who's not a Navajo. Harmony is a key element of the Dineh philosophy known as the Beauty Way.

" 'I'll use an example,' he says. 'Terrible drought. Crops dead. Sheep dying. Spring dried out. No water. The Hopi, or the Christian, maybe the Moslem, they pray for rain. The Navajo has the proper ceremony done to restore himself to harmony with the drought. You see what I mean? The system is designed to recognize what's beyond human power to change, and then to change the human's attitude to be content with the inevitable.' "

———————

In March 2003 I wake up one Sunday morning in a body that's become a foreign country. Weapons of mass destruction have been released inside my mouth. My tongue and mucous membranes are covered with painful sores, and there's a strange taste I can't identify because I've never experienced it before.

I haven't got the energy to get out of bed. And this is just the beginning of chemo. It's supposed to get progressively worse. In the course of half a day, I take two naps. Finally I can't stand it anymore and force myself to get up and go for a walk.

I go to Dimond Park, in the Fruitvale district. There's a trail that winds along the course of Sausal Creek, which is in the process of being restored to a native plant habitat.

I force my legs to keep moving. Past the beginning of the trail there's a crosswalk into Dimond Canyon. Immediately there's a whole new world. Trees arch in a sylvan canopy over the burbling creek. Splotches of sunlight dapple the green. There's a hush so profound you can hardly believe you're in Oakland, land of drug turf killings and screeching sideshow cars. On the soft path, my legs begin to move on their own. I take in the copious green, the still silence, the movement of the water. My head clears, and a sweeping happiness rises inside me.

It's not a very long walk, about half an hour, half what I usually do. But I am so thoroughly refreshed that when I return home, I begin writing. I write for hours. By the time I go to bed I'm feeling happy and fulfilled.

This is a major lesson I'm learning about my disease and its treatment. Everything changes moment by moment. Forget one day at a time. One day is too large an increment in which to measure the changes.

It's almost impossible to make plans. Monday I have a perfectly normal day. I'm planning to go to my friend Kate Coleman's for dinner. But around six I'm hit with a wave of nausea and a sudden fever. I definitely can't drive.

As a way-past-menopausal hot flasher I could go nearly the whole winter without turning on the heat in my house. Now I have the heat on full blast, and I'm wrapped in a cashmere shawl. Kate has brought the food to my house.

"Wow," she says, "it's really hot in here."

This is something almost no one has ever said about my house.

I've bought a digital thermometer to take my temperature. It measures 100.9. The point at which you're supposed to call the advice nurse at Kaiser is 101 degrees. I don't call. The mouth sores plague me. That is another symptom I'm supposed to report but haven't yet done.

Tuesday morning I feel great. I go for my weekly walk in Redwood Park with Judy Mollica. We call ourselves cancer pals. She has multiple myeloma, though her disease so far is still in the "smoldering stage." We talk about everything on our walks, which follow the west ridge over French Creek, through redwood groves and fragrant bay trees, past long vistas across the canyon over ridges colored in soft grays and blues, like Chinese inkwash paintings.

I go home for lunch, then drive to Pleasanton. I have an errand to do at 2 the Point, a needlepoint store. I feel great.

Until six, when I'm suddenly hit by a wave of nausea and a fever that this time reaches 101.

It's too bad Franz Kafka didn't live in the right time to be a

Kaiser member because he would have had a picnic with the phone system.

Dr. Gordon, my oncologist, agrees about the phone system. "It's our Achilles' heel," he says.

As I discover anyhow, the best way to communicate with Dr. Gordon is through e-mail. He's accessible to answer questions by e-mail or see me on short notice when something goes wrong.

Which of course it does. My mouth sores become so bad that the pain is excruciating. Every morning, when the sores are at their worst, I stand in my kitchen weeping, trying one thing and then another to make the pain go away. I have something the oncology pharmacist has given me, called magic mouthwash, that numbs the pain, but only for moments.

I have to use the mouthwash before I can eat anything. I'm hungry, but the minute food touches my cheeks or my tongue, it feels as though someone has taken a blowtorch to the inside of my mouth. Eating is a torment. So is talking. I have to teach a knitting class and can hardly bear to speak to the students.

I have numbing throat sprays, licorice pills, saltwater rinses; nothing works for long. Some of the sores begin to ulcerate and form craters inside the back of my mouth. The pain intensifies. In desperation I hire a psychic healer and go see a Chinese dermatology specialist.

The Chinese doctor, Jialing Yu, gives me mouthwash and powders. They are based on an herb called watermelon frost. Finally, they provide some relief.

The psychic healer helps my energy return to normal.

At my breast cancer support group, Kathie Weston, a cofacilitator, asks how I'm doing since I started chemotherapy, and I burst into tears. "I don't think Dr. Gordon is really hearing you," she says. "I don't think he is hearing how bad you feel."

Fired up from the group, I come home and write Dr. Gordon an e-mail so acerbic that I think he will fire me as a patient. The next morning his nurse calls and says he wants to see me. At last he looks inside my mouth.

"Oh," he says, "I see what you mean."

He tells me that patients normally don't develop such bad mucositis, the official name for this malady, and urges me to take pain pills. The pain pills present another problem for me. I can't stand the feeling of being impaired. I can't drive, can't write, can't think, can't even do my needlework. But at least I don't have pain.

Between the Chinese powders, the ministrations of the psychic healer, and the curative power of time away from the chemo infusions, my mouth sores begin to heal. Dr. Gordon suggests that perhaps I chew ice chips during the next infusion to prevent them. We have been having a lively e-mail exchange about preventions, cures, and various types of research. The ice chip treatment is known as cryotherapy, a fancy name for a simple homemade remedy.

It works. After my second treatment, I am more tired and nauseated for several days following the infusion, more debilitated. But the mouth sores never blossom into the full-blown anguish they were the first time.

I have no hair. Rather, I am bald with stubble. I got my hair cut short after beginning chemo, so that when it started falling out, it wouldn't be such a shock. Still, when clumps of it begin raining down in the shower, I am horrified. The bottom of my bathtub looks like that Frida Kahlo painting where she has cut off her hair and heaps of it, like bunched-up iron filings, lie all over the floor.

Every time a bunch of hair goes toward the drain I scoop it up and throw it away. But I can't keep up with it, and there is something about it that is so disturbing on a primal level that I begin to cry uncontrollably.

After I get out of the shower, my daughter calls on the phone. I am crying, so she asks my friend Natalie to come over. Natalie brings a beautiful scarf, which she arranges on me in a dramatic head wrap. A few days later, when Ishi comes over for the morning to play Scrabble, I ask Rune to buzz my scalp.

Now I look like a chemotherapy patient. I wear scarves and hats. A friend has given me a soft cotton cap, like a baby's hat, to sleep in. My head is cold at night without hair. Linda from the Knitting Basket makes me a silk chenille beret. It's quite an honor; I've never had anything she knitted before. I knit myself a silk and wool "origami hat" in an electrifying shade of magenta, from a kit Cheryl Oberle sends me from Colorado. She says the silk will feel good against my scalp.

Still, it is a shock to my image and something of an identity crisis. One friend says, "It is a small price to pay." Everyone says it will eventually grow back. No matter what anyone else thinks about it, though, it is a startling thing to look in the mirror and behold yourself bald.

The duration of chemotherapy treatments is objectively really short. But it seems to stretch out interminably. I realize I am hunkered down in raw survival mode, waiting for it to be over. Two weeks feels like five years.

My body is not my own. Neither is the face I see in the mirror. I have little energy and must guard it carefully for what I have to do. Simple tasks take twice as long. My mind is otherwise engaged; I feel absentminded and dull-witted. I can't knit anything complicated. That requires too much attention. I can't write either; often I'm at a loss for words.

I do needlepoint and read. Whatever shreds of my life BBC, as I call it (before breast cancer), that can be salvaged during this time constitute a major victory. Walks with Judy Mollica are a lifeline. Other friends bring food, offer rides, help, companionship. This is not the life I'm accustomed to. I'm used to being pushed by my job, my need to accomplish hundreds of tasks in the course of a week, to being energetic and independent.

Now I'm a cancer patient. I'm slowed way down. Everything in my life is reduced to bare-bones simplicity. I need to rest a lot and let other people do things for me. One bonus is that my daughter begins to spend more time with me. She brings over groceries, cooks dinner, does dishes, and watches TV with me. We watch the good

Sunday night HBO shows and laugh together at reruns of *Friends*. We are closer and more intimate than we have been in years.

I find that simple, ordinary life, with all its quotidian details, becomes the most precious time I have. That might not be everyone's experience, but it is mine.

———

Chemotherapy has its own cycle. For the first few days after the infusion I can hardly do anything. Then I begin to bounce back. At some time during the middle of the three-week break, my blood count drops, and I'm debilitated again. Then my energy returns. By the time the next treatment is near I feel almost normal.

The one thing I know is that everything passes. If I feel bad, I know it will pass. If I feel good, I know it will pass. Everything changes. Though it feels as though I've been in this darkness for a million years, some part of me knows that sooner or later it's going to end.

———

Midway through the three-week cycle between chemo treatments, an event occurs that oncologists refer to as the nadir. This is the point at which the patient's blood count drops the lowest. Theoretically, another chemotherapy infusion cannot be administered until the blood count comes back up.

So far my blood counts had been fine, but shortly before the third treatment was due to occur, I hit a point I thought of as an emotional nadir.

My spirits suddenly dropped so low that I began to feel as though I were battling my old enemy, depression, as much as I was battling my current enemy, breast cancer.

Without my normal amount of energy, I had a hard time keeping active enough to stave off depression. And I spent so much time resting and alone that I had begun to engage in a fair amount of reviewing and analysis of my life.

Since my ideas about love were tied up with my feelings for my father, and since I believed that Billy was my last chance at love, I felt as though I were giving up the possibility of romantic love. At least I was giving up the view of romantic love I had held since adolescence, if not before. The letting go, I believe, dovetailed with the sadness part of grieving my father's death, the stage where you finally accept that the person is gone and that you are never going to see him or her again in this life.

Between my father, Judith, and the other losses I had borne, I felt as though I were surrounded by death. All the people in my life who had been present and suddenly disappeared began to haunt me. With my cancer diagnosis, I was facing my own death as well.

What did it all mean? I wondered. How do you live knowing you are going to die? Facing your own mortality with a life-threatening illness, how do you change your life so that you are finally living the life that you want, however brief it may turn out to be?

15. Tangled Up in Blue

CHEMOTHERAPY DEMANDED ALL MY POWERS OF SUR-
vival to endure. "The beauty of my characters is that
they endure," William Faulkner once said. "May we
endure," Ray toasted Inna, Judith's gardener and
friend, himself, and me as we gathered to celebrate
Judith's sixtieth birthday in the spring after she died.

During chemo I stopped almost everything I
had done before and became unable to write. All I
could do was endure. Radiation as well demanded so
much of me that I simplified my life and did as little
as possible.

I rested all afternoon after radiation. I began
playing cards on my computer. I think I was trying to
get my brain back to functioning. Betty Grant of the
Knitting Basket told me that a dear friend of hers had

played a lot of computer bridge after completing chemotherapy and had gone on to win master points in tournaments.

Bridge is an activity that seems to open neural pathways in different parts of the brain, to deal with spatial relationships, memorization of all the cards played, strategies, and counterstrategies. After bridge, I began to play Payday Free Cell, a complex form of solitaire that seemed almost like an IQ test. Each hand was a puzzle that needed to be solved. There was one card that held the secret to unraveling the puzzle, the one that would cause all the rest of the cards to fly into formation for a win. The key was to uncover that card and get everything else ready for when it emerged.

I became so addicted to this game of solitaire that I began to fear for my so-called sanity. Sometimes, though I am embarrassed to admit this, I stayed up till all hours, eating sunflower seeds until my mouth was raw, and woke up feeling as though I'd been out on a drug binge or terrific drunk.

There is a phenomenon known as chemo brain. Cancer patients, particularly breast cancer patients, often report that their mental functioning becomes impaired. They lose memory, have problems with word retrieval, feel confused and disoriented. Jane Brody once reported in the *New York Times* that up to 30 percent of breast cancer patients experience some degree of permanent cognitive dysfunction following chemotherapy.

Conversely, studies have shown that contract bridge improves cognitive function and helps in the conservation of mental acuity in older women who play regularly. So I think in some way I was trying to rescue my mind from the ravages of chemotherapy.

I had been terrified of this particular side effect when starting chemo. "I can't think straight," I complained to Dr. Gordon when my treatments were over. "I have problems remembering words. I can't write."

For the two years before my cancer diagnosis, I had been writing a three-times-weekly column in the *Oakland Tribune*. I had hoped that column writing would make me prolific, and it had. I still procrastinated before I wrote, but with the exigencies of daily newspaper deadlines, opportunities to stall were severely limited. So I went into my writing tunnel and wrote.

I wrote in the midst of total chaos, surrounded by people, conversations, breaking news, dramas left and right. Once I entered the tunnel, all other sensory stimulation fell away. There was a lot of private pleasure for me in the writing of these columns. By private pleasure, I mean getting something exactly right, whether it was the distinctive voice of a subject, a particular sentence, or the delineation of a complicated concept in the abbreviated form of a newspaper story.

Tom Sawyer, a crusty old newspaper veteran I worked with on the paper before his retirement, liked to tell reporters, "The invasion of Normandy was written in eight inches."

Writing is writing. All writing is practice and involves the solving of certain technical problems. All of it requires the carving out of a recognizable shape from raw material with lapidary care. With my column, I liked having an available forum to comment on what was happening in the present. There was very little distance between initial conception and publication, which was unusual in my experience.

But I missed the more ruminative sort of writing I was accustomed to doing. The descent into deep contemplation of a subject. The feeling I sometimes had when engaged in writing a book that I had fallen into a state of grace.

In many ways I measured my self-worth by writing. Knitting and needlepoint were what I did; writing was who I was. I had grown used to long periods of time between writing projects, times when I doubted I would, or could, ever write again. I seemingly could not predict when it would begin anew, or control its ebb and flow. Though writing wasn't pleasant for me, it was always a pleasure when the discipline returned, when I became submerged in something I knew would require years to complete. Between times, I made pillows and sweaters, needlepoint pictures, and intricate, lacy shawls.

Of course it could be argued that I might have written more if I hadn't spent so much time knitting.

"How come I never wrote a book before?" I asked my old boyfriend Max, who lived with me in New York in the 1970s.

"You did," he said. "But they didn't publish sweaters."

———

The doctors had convinced me I had a good chance of being cured if I went through the aggressive treatments. Midway through the chemo, it seemed as though these treatments would never end.

Throughout my younger life I had struggled with depression. In this case, combined with a loss of energy, it came to seem even more terrifying.

I could go through the motions of needlepoint, knitting, reading, seeing friends, taking care of my everyday existence, but the joy began seeping out of all that I did.

Most of the women in my breast cancer support group were married and spoke often about their husbands. Married people seemed like an alien species to me. How did they stay with one person through a whole lifetime? Coexist in the same living space? What did they know that I didn't?

Many women in the group had been the caretakers in their families, the eldest of multiple children, the person in the family to whom everyone else brought his or her problems. Many had suffered big personal losses in the two years preceding the cancer.

I bounced back and forth between believing that the breast cancer was simply the result of exposure to environmental toxins, or the product of a faulty DNA mechanism, and suspecting that it had a psychological cause and had come as a result of certain patterns in my life. Caretaking was one of them. Betraying myself by living a life not suited to my core self was another.

Grieving seemed as though it might be another underlying

cause of the cancer. Was there a better way to mourn that I didn't know, just as there must be a better way to love that I didn't know?

These were some of the questions that nagged at me as I sank into the emotional nadir of my chemotherapy cycle.

———

When you look at a raw needlepoint canvas, it can seem like an unsolvable puzzle, thick and overwhelming. You cannot imagine where to begin or how to proceed.

It is only when you actually take the plunge, stitching the first stitch, that you see where the next one will lead, and the next one, and the one after that. You can't see much beyond one stitch at a time. But you can see that.

It was the way I had to proceed through chemotherapy. In my body, which felt as though it had been invaded by aliens, I had to proceed one step at a time. I couldn't look too far ahead or attempt to see the big picture.

My life itself had become a needlepoint canvas. An impenetrable thicket. Full of holes.

———

My nearly weekly bridge games, a remnant of my precancer life, came to seem like a blessing to me. The strategies and stratagems of contract bridge occupied my mind completely and distracted me from the business at hand, which was increasingly unpleasant to contemplate.

During one of our bridge games a special about Joni Mitchell aired on public TV. In the quest for love and for understanding of love, Joni Mitchell had been like an interior companion for me. "My favorite subject," she once told an interviewer, "is disappointment in love."

The special focused on Mitchell's early work, the days when she had, to employ the cliché, spoken for a generation. Many songs that had consoled me through personal heartache—"Blue," "A Case of You," "I Wish I Had a River"—were played on the show.

Like me, Mitchell focused on two separate areas of creativity. Mine were knitting and writing. Hers were music and painting. During times of composing, she ceased to paint, and she used painting to replenish her resources after she had depleted them by composing. In an interview she recalled a time she had become so distraught by the events and circumstances of her life that she retreated to the Canadian wilderness to gather her thoughts and put her shattered emotions in order.

During this time, she said, she had fought depression. "But what's so bad about depression?" she asked. "Depression can be the grain of sand that makes the pearl inside the oyster."

Though her work had so often focused on romantic love, it was clear that the force that had sustained her through a long and interesting life was her drive toward self-expression, her passionate need to create. In this, also, I felt a kinship with her.

Joni Mitchell's songs had wound in and out of the lives of my family. My brother, Ricky, who may have been partially inspired to become a composer himself by Mitchell's example, was so enamored of her at one point that he made her a hand-embroidered floor-length dress.

After I wrote an article about Mitchell, she and my brother corresponded for a time. At a concert in New York, during which she recognized Ricky from the stage, he put the full-length dress, wrapped in a package tied with string, on the stage.

I wish the story had a happier ending, but he never heard from her again. The dress? Lost to history.

There is a set of symptoms in the study of homeopathy, the system of complementary medicine practiced by my sister Lorraine as well as by my longtime physician Ellen Gunther, that includes the description "improved by music." I took that to mean a general lifting of the spirits that happened whenever certain types of music were played.

Whatever was wrong with me, and had been wrong for most of my adult life, could have included the description "improved by music." The musicians and songwriters who accompanied my generation's passage through the 1960s and 1970s, who continue on the journey with us till the present day, gave words to the inchoate yearnings and heartsickness that possessed us. They lessened the heartbreaks, amplified the hopes, beat the drums for various convictions and causes, and gave voice to our shared experience.

The foremost of these for me was Bob Dylan. And I could say during this time that my feelings were not only improved but best described by one of my favorites of his songs: "Like a bird that flew, tangled up in blue."

16. Steeped
in Judith

DURING MY EMOTIONAL NADIR FROM THE CHEMOTHER-
apy treatments, I went to Judith's house to go
through her clothes and try to find some keepsakes
to take away. It had been about six months since her
death. Ray had been inviting some of Judith's close
friends over, in an attempt to dispose of the overwhelming number of personal possessions left behind
and to give us something to remember her by.

I went with Inna, the gardener, who had been
as close to Judith as anyone besides her sister and
Ray. Bettina had already come from the East Coast
and gone through her sister's sweaters. A friend from
Paris had also come, with her daughter, and taken
back suitcases filled with Judith's things.

Inna told me that the Paris friend, Dorian, had

found the place in Judith's closet where she had hidden the gun. Judith's clothes were in two large closets in the side room she used for her study. Hundreds of pairs of shoes covered the floors of the closets and were stacked on the high shelves. In among the boxes of shoes, Dorian had found a paper bag containing the gun license, bullets, and presumably the gun, which the police had taken away.

Judith seemed to have kept everything she had ever owned. Her closet was so packed with dresses from the 1960s, 1970s, 1980s, 1990s, and present that one could scarcely get anything in or out. It reminded me of a somewhat humorous article I had written for the *Village Voice* years before about a revival of true preppy style. "The rich are different from you and me," the article began. "They have more closet space."

Judith's possessions certainly bore that out. Ray had printed up a program for a memorial service at a Friends' meetinghouse in Berkeley that showed a photo of Judith in a sun hat, taken on the beach in Quogue, on Long Island, in 1976. The sun hat was still among her things. I searched my mind to see if I still owned anything I had had in 1976, and the list was short indeed.

There were original Puccis, Sonia Rykiel dresses short enough to look like tops, Helga Howie designs, Missoni tops and skirts, hundreds of patterned rayon day dresses and linen jumpers for summer. The ladylike clothes she had favored—like a short-sleeved white linen dress with buttons down the front, hung in the closet with its own slip—would have been at home with spectator pumps at a Southampton garden party.

In the bedroom, sweaters were stacked on shelves, along with cotton blouses and dozens of ironed white cotton nightgowns.

Inna and I began looking through the dresses. Judith had been slender and fine-boned, and it quickly became clear that there was nothing among the dresses that would fit me.

I chose to take a soft and well-worn flannel bathrobe, along with a Liberty lawn blouse of the sort we had worn in college more than four decades before. I also took a sweater that still smelled like Judith, which I found comforting, and some necklaces and things for Shuna and Marilyn. Many more things fitted Inna; she seemed as well to possess more stamina and desire to look.

The trouble was that I could feel Judith in the study. She inhabited the room, the clothes, the sweaters and shoes. Judith had been a strong presence, serious and commanding, and her often proper mode of dressing was distinctive, to say the least, in bohemian Berkeley. I was haunted as well by the nearness of the bullets. I couldn't help wondering about the last moments of Judith's life, when and why she had decided to take the gun down from the shelf, load the bullets, put her plan into sudden, irrevocable action.

Anyone who has meditated or done any sort of spiritual studies knows that money and material possessions are not the secret of happiness. But for those of us who have suffered through financial worries and material deprivation, the illusion persists that satisfaction of one's every desire would surely ensure *some* happiness in life.

Judith had a life second to none. Yearly trips to New York, to Florence and Venice, to London and Paris, with money to buy whatever she wanted, and the taste, intelligence, and culture to pursue the best the civilized world had to offer. With the exquisite home one of Inna's friends called the villa, the flourishing garden, the well-tended marriage of thirty-five years' duration. With the humanitarian work, the devotion to liberal causes, the impeccably planned parties and benefits, the cultivated circle of friends.

We were in the midst of the material proof of Judith's plenty, the dresses and shoes and sweaters and gowns. I could feel her floating around in the study, dressing herself, in her quiet, serious, determined way. She was not showy, was more low-key and offhand in her manner, though elegant and stylish.

I could feel her in the room, reaching up into her closet, taking down the hidden gun, the secret vehicle of destruction. They all meant nothing to her. The gardens, the home, the clothes, the travel, the marriage, the friends, the good works, the puppy she had recently obtained.

I began a poem when Judith died. "What did you think with your hand on the trigger? Were you thinking that soon you'd be freed of your pain?" I could not conjure up the agony or decision of those last desperate moments. I could not imagine the perseverance or psychosis that enabled her to pull the trigger, to end it all so violently that those of us around her are still in shock and will be left reeling for years.

At almost every gathering of Judith's friends and loved ones, we speak of nothing else. Out of consideration to Ray, there are things we don't talk about when he is around. It took months for Inna to summon up the courage to tell him the gun had been hidden in the closet, amid the boxes of shoes.

After a few hours among Judith's things, I had to leave. I was already struggling with sadness and lack of energy, and it was strange to be going through such intimate parts of my lost friend's life. I later found out that the box wrapped in a silk scarf that sat atop her painted dresser held her ashes, her earthly remains.

Did we have her permission to go through her things? Did she mind? Would she care? Is she still around? Where do we go when we die, the strong presence that is our blood and bones and hearts and minds? Do we vanish off the face of the earth or stay close to our loved ones in a more invisible form?

As usual, I had no answers to my questions. All I knew at the end of that day was that I felt as though I had been steeped in Judith. Her presence had been both disturbing and comforting, her ultimate actions puzzling and incomprehensible.

I deeply loved Judith. On the occasion of that September dinner we had acted like lovers out on our first date, lingering first one place and then another to keep from bidding each other good-bye. I felt so much tenderness toward her. I knew her vulnerability and her pain and yet, like all her friends, could do nothing really to help her or save her.

Judith gave all her friends a social life. She was a meticulous and prolific planner of events, a hostess of fabulous parties. She celebrated every occasion with dinners, presents, phone calls, and dates. Ray says she planned their entire travel itineraries, for all the trips they took.

Two weeks before she died, Judith threw a dinner party for Ray's and my shared birthday. She gave me a lovely jade teacup, with a saucer and cover to match. Inna remembers her telegraphing her intentions, announcing to me that the jade cup was my Christmas present as well. I don't remember; I wasn't aware. Though Judith seemed more subdued than usual, a little puffy from medication she had recently started, nothing in her behavior made me suspect that in two weeks she'd be gone.

Once she was here, and very much here. Now she is gone, and very much gone. Her death, like my father's, is an inescapable certainty.

Knowing that, how do we go on? How do we live in the presence of death? That's really the only question.

17. Everything Is Water

RADIATION FOLLOWS CHEMOTHERAPY AS DARKNESS FOL-
lows light. It occupies most of the summer. The
morning after radiation ends, I wake up to an unfa-
miliar smell. Ozone. Incredibly for Northern California, it has rained in late July. The ground is soaked
from the night before.

I wish the rain could wash me clean. I've been
cut, poisoned, and burned, and it's not over yet.

Lately I've been irritable and grouchy. My tol-
erance for frustration is low. I know I have to make a
new life for myself yet again. It took a while for the
breast cancer treatments to sweep away my regular
life; now they are over, and I have to start anew. I've
always considered myself adaptable, but I don't turn
on a dime.

The abyss of depression yawns in front of me. Perhaps I've already fallen in and don't know it. Some friends complain about my "negativity," as though one should remain cheerful and upbeat through the sheer hell of breast cancer treatment.

A strange fact of life is that even the most unpleasant things, once they stop, require a period of mourning. Or they need to be replaced. I can imagine the life I'd like to have for myself. Restore my vitality with long walks. Write. Take up some challenging knitting project again.

I've signed up for individual therapy with one of the cofacilitators of my support group. In the intake interview, one of the doctors asks me, "Are you deriving less enjoyment from your activities?"

Hell, yes.

I'm barely knitting. I'm apathetic playing bridge with friends. Even my latest obsession, playing bridge online on Pogo, has ceased to provide me much pleasure. More often it's upsetting and frustrating. Other players make me angry and on occasion even bring me to tears.

I have a strange pain in my elbow, which I'm sure is incipient bone cancer, a metastasis from the breast tumor. From what I've seen in my support group, this is fairly common. Once you've lost your innocence in this area, each new ache and pain, each headache, each neurological nuance is proof that the cancer has spread.

The dread word *recurrence* occurs more and more often in the breast cancer support group, which has now grown so big that the counselors have split it in two. Women diagnosed more than eighteen months ago will form a new group. I'm sure it's because the counselors are convinced that sooner or later one of us is going to have a recurrence.

Those of us who are newer are still reeling from the diagnosis and treatments. The treatments often seem worse than the disease. I have trouble keeping in mind that the breast cancer actually threatened my life.

At the same time I've done virtually nothing else for the past seven months but deal with this one way or another.

Now what? I struggle to remember what my life was like before breast cancer.

I was a driven type A personality, sort of like my dad. I rushed through days that sometimes lasted twelve hours. I crammed as many activities as could possibly fit into each single day.

Once the breast cancer treatments started, I had to take the opposite tack. Now I did as few activities as possible in the greatest number of hours.

At one time or another I did a daily forty-five-minute meditation that anchored the day. Throughout the course of treatment I continued to do needlepoint. It was soothing and pleasantly relaxing.

Knitting seemed too complex. It involved thinking, planning, mathematical calculations. It involved more concentration than I could muster.

Needlepoint was just what the doctor ordered, the doctor being me. It contained within it the pure pleasures of color and pattern. To get the same variety of color and pictorial quality in knitting, you'd have to do intarsia, which I don't like. Each change of color requires so many steps, so many constrictions, that I feel imprisoned and unfree.

In needlepoint you change color whenever you want. The simple rhythm of the stitches provides a childish delight.

Oddly, many of the needlepoint scenes I stitched while undergoing treatment for breast cancer turned out to be underwater scenes. To complete those canvases, I have to depict the big water, a stitch at a time, a spray at a time, to feel the fish swim through a liquid medium, created by an illusion made of thread.

I wonder when my mother fell in love with needlepoint. Her greatest pride is her needlepoint pillows. She says it takes her six to nine months to finish each one. I'm such a maniac that I am now completing large canvases, with smaller holes and finer thread than my mother uses, in two months or less.

Like knitting, it is a miracle of thread.

I watch a spider ascending on her invisible web through what seems like thin air and think about miracles of thread. I have a hard time killing spiders, vastly preferring to trap them and take them outside. What I do is so much like what they do that my feeling of kinship overrides my fear of them and the horror that they are living inside my house.

The spider can ride to heaven on a web that she spins even as she goes. Though domestic evidence would seem to prove that she needs a solid surface from which to begin her ascent or descent.

There are scary spiders where I live. Brown recluses whose bite can kill or cause incredible pain. "I'd rather deliver twins vaginally," said my friend Lee Ann, after being bitten by a brown recluse in West Marin. We also have black widows. And less poisonous spiders whose bites can still cause swelling or pain.

How nice to think they're roommates, sharing my intimate living space with me.

———

I've thought a lot about both my parents during the long months of radiation. I think of my father and his changing obsessions, his "hobbies," as we called them at the time. For years he rode horses, talked about horses, dreamed of having his own horse farm. Then it was over, and his interest vanished as though it had never been there. Same with racing pigeons. Same with fishing boats. Same with oil paintings.

Nowadays we call these things passions. We "follow our bliss." I bristle when I hear my needlework described as a hobby; it seems like so much more to me.

But I'm every bit as helpless over my changing obsessions as my father was. I can lose interest in something I formerly loved in a hot minute and never want to go back to it again. I can be overtaken by a new love to the point where it drives everything else from my life.

Before my bout with breast cancer, I imagined that an encounter with life-threatening illness would leave me more appreciative of the preciousness of life. Instead it seemed to do the opposite, leveling everything out and neutralizing it. If life indeed is short and uncertain, I reasoned, it really doesn't matter what I do. Might as well play bridge on Pogo for an abstract numerical rating as put an end to world hunger or write the great American novel.

The leveling feeling reminds me of the line of a Robert Creeley poem, "Just Friends," that I've always liked: "Everything is water if you look long enough."

I don't know if what I feel is depression or detachment, a hell of suffering or a sudden glimpse of enlightenment.

Indulging in this point of view, I am completely demoralized by the time radiation ends. The women in my support group assure me this is perfectly normal, though it appears to be an aberration. Like so much else in the trajectory of breast cancer treatments, it comes as an anomaly, an unexpected result. I thought I would be happy when treatment was over; instead I'm distraught.

Many who survive life-threatening illness report that the experience makes them value their lives. They learn to treasure each moment, they say. My experience is the opposite. I watched my father go from life to death, stared into the face of death, survived a deadly form of cancer. Yet far from feeling as though every golden moment were a precious gift, I feel it doesn't matter what I do.

The needlepoint sort of goes with this. It has no earthly use—there is a limit to how many pillows one can fit inside a one-bedroom house already stuffed to bursting with bags of yarn—and is purely decorative in nature. It is neither goal-oriented nor productive in any sense of the word. Yet paradoxically it has ensured my survival.

Even the needlepoint, however, can't keep me from depression once the treatment ends. Then one day, as fate would have it, I go where I've always gone for consolation: to the knitting store.

There is a large hank of laceweight wool and silk I've had my eye on for a while. It is hand-painted in shades of blue, all the blues of the ocean, from the deepest navy to the palest sky blue. I find a pattern for a simple lace shawl in the new Rowan book.

I buy the yarn and begin knitting. Immediately my depression starts to lift. Any knitter will recognize the truth of this, I think, though it sounds almost unbelievable.

As I work on the triangular lace shawl in the colors of the ocean, I knit into my imagination the feel of the water, the measure of its depth. Will it fall over my shoulders like a cooling mantle when it is finished? Will it match my internal emotional reality, reflect my body of water?

I knit and I wonder. Is God a knitter, a craftsperson, a seamstress? Did (s)he create the vast oceans with a sweep of the hand or patiently construct them one drop at a time? The most miraculous things in the world are those we totally take for granted: water and skin. Who could dream of constructing a seamless, elastic, self-repairing fabric of any fiber available on earth? Who could synthesize the proper combination of hydrogen and oxygen to produce a substance that boils and freezes, moves violently of its own accord, cuts through rock and gently soaks tiny plants, or bursts dams and levels whole villages and towns. I contemplate the miracles of water and skin as yarn passes through my fingers, on its way to creating a garment of softness and warmth.

I think about the break I had from knitting. Had I hit some sort of wall before it? I had achieved what I set out to do twelve years ago, to master the techniques that interested me, to understand the intricacies of fit and form. I became current in knitting; I knew the latest yarn, the newest patterns, whatever was most up-to-date in the knitting universe. Perhaps, I thought, there was noplace left to go.

I hadn't reckoned on the pure pleasure of starting a new rhythmic pattern of lace, of increasing, decreasing, forming a picture with fullness and emptiness, creating a delicate, gossamer shape.

Knitting the lace feels like recovering a piece of myself that's been lost for a while. My heart and imagination soar. I begin to be happy.

So I've come home to knitting, though I still can't write.

———

I don't believe there's a heaven, an afterlife for the good, a paradise of sensual pleasure that the bad are forbidden. I believe in the life that lives in the universe and the sky. I believe we are connected to a larger whole, that we contain within ourselves a spark of divinity. I believe we reincarnate from one body to another, cycling through history and time.

Sometimes after chemotherapy I would go with Lou to the

ocean in Pacifica. We would walk on the pier and watch the waves break. At a certain close distance from the water, I always begin to feel better, energized, revitalized, cleansed, and revived by the salt air.

The ocean contains within itself that mysterious, humbling vastness and volition. Watching the ocean swell and crash gives one a sense of space, openness, power, depth, the long view to the horizon, the endlessness of movement.

If I am cremated, I would like my ashes to be scattered in the water in Hawaii. Perhaps on Makena Beach on Maui, or near Napoopoo Beach on the Big Island, in Kealakekua Bay, where Captain Cook met his doom. I'd like to spend eternity, if there is such a thing, submerged in the healing waters. If I have to lose my earthly form, and all of us do, then let me be part of the ocean, a droplet of water in the sea.

18. Visibility: Unlimited

September 2003

OPPORTUNITIES FOR HEALING ABOUND IN THE UNIVERSE if you know just where to look. Sick to death of medical intervention after surgery, chemo, and radiation, I embarked on my own healing journey.

First I purchased a spectacular needlepoint canvas. It was a picture of a dragon's face or the head of a lion from the Chinese New Year parade. Whatever it was, it breathed fire. It existed on a field of red so red that I considered the color medicinal in and of itself.

If I immersed myself in this red, I thought, breathed it, touched it, absorbed it, it might bring vitality back to my body. I didn't do tai chi anymore. I was lazy about my body. The workings of my hands and mind engaged me so much more.

The red background of the needlepoint was the red of a cardinal's feathers, the crimson of stoplights reflected in puddles, of floppy hibiscus flowers in the tropics, fire engines, scarlet satin, rubies, salvia, rouge. It was a red so luscious you could taste its cherry tartness in your mouth.

Its color reminded me of a favorite Grateful Dead song, "Scarlet Begonias," that Jerry Garcia sang with a poignant catch in his voice, placing it squarely in some imaginary mythical world. Not that I'm proud to be a Deadhead at this age. But it happens.

There's a line in this song I quote in my epigraph: "Once in a while, you get shown the light in the strangest of places, if you look at it right." I've experienced the truth of this in those rare moments when the veil of illusion suddenly parts and the light of pure consciousness emerges from behind.

As the Buddhists say, you still chop wood and carry water, but somehow, subtly, you know things have changed.

My experience of this, at least so far, is that the state of awareness is not solidly present in me all the time. It comes and goes as it pleases. Once it has been there, however, the possibility of its existence has been established, and there's no going back.

Along with the reds, I gathered threads in shaded variations of other colors for the rest of the lion's head. I was planning to take the whole thing to Wyoming, where I had an upcoming residency at the Ucross Foundation, an artists' colony. Sharon Dynak, the Ucross director, was kind enough to offer me another time slot when I had to cancel due to breast cancer treatments.

Sandy Walker, an Oakland artist I once interviewed for my newspaper column, spent several residencies at Ucross and painted numerous depictions of what he saw.

One painting was an arrangement of four squares: the dun color of the hills, the blue of the sky, the green of the cottonwoods, and a vivid red like the red of my needlepoint, not the darker red that gives the Ucross barn and gallery their name, Big Red.

Walker also painted the unique shapes of the cottonwoods in different arrangements of those four colors. Seeing those paintings was one of my inspirations to apply to Ucross. My brother's having been there sealed the deal.

I believe we have a need for space, physical space around us, as great as our need for food and water.

Ucross sits in the middle of twenty-two thousand acres, in northeastern Wyoming, the least populous state in the nation. Population density in Wyoming adds up to about five persons per square mile. A working cattle ranch, Ucross is located in the arid Powder River basin. Typically it receives less than twelve inches of water a year. Yet paradoxically the land was once the bottom of a huge inland lake, and the landscape resembles an undulating sea bottom, with craggy protrusions and wind-eroded buttes. On some of the hills, seashells are embedded in the scoria, the coal-rich rock.

In early September, when I arrived in Wyoming, everything surrounding Ucross was the dun color of dried grass, except for the vivid green of the regularly watered lawns of the foundation and the darker green of the alfalfa fields.

A man named Keith, of the Ucross staff, picked me up at the airport. I took as a good omen the sight that greeted my eyes in the Gillette-Campbell County Airport, a huge diorama of a Plains Indian on horseback, bow and arrow drawn, chasing down a running buffalo. It is one of four large, meticulously rendered scenes of Wyoming wildlife, featuring a giant elk, pronghorn antelope, prairie dogs, and prairie chickens. But the Indian, who wears a green painted shirt and rides a painted pony, was a vision to gladden my heart.

As Keith drove toward Ucross, a beautiful golden hawk flew right past the windshield. The second day I was there, for the first time in my life I saw sandhill cranes.

"Do you hear that sound?" asked Ruthie, the resident chef.

It was a strange sort of burbling sound above us, too loud to come from a bird the size of a dove, not quite the squawkings of geese.

"It's the sandhill cranes. They've been hanging around here all summer." There were some flying above us, with their enormous wingspans and their gliding stops; some were already out in the field.

———

I loved that part of the universe. The Powder River country was the homeland of Crazy Horse, the great Sioux warrior and mystic, who wanted his reservation there. The Fetterman Massacre, in which Crazy Horse acted as a decoy, one of his earliest military exploits, took place not far from Ucross, in Storey, Wyoming. The Wagon Box Fight, another Crazy Horse battle, also took place nearby. And the Little Bighorn Battlefield, site of Custer's Last Stand, is in southeastern Montana, only about twenty minutes' drive from Ucross.

So the land was rich in history, with tepee circles and medicine wheels. It was also rich in wildlife. At any moment you might encounter pronghorn antelope, a flock of wild turkeys, whitetail and mule deer, sandhill cranes, beaver, prairie dogs, muskrats, hawks, a golden eagle or an osprey. I watched for rattlesnakes when I walked across the fields. I looked for sightings of elk, bear, moose, wolves, coyotes, and mountain lions on an excursion to the Bighorn Mountains. Though I didn't actually see them, it was a comfort to know they were close by.

It's a lonely world without animals, once you have removed them from the land you inhabit. I don't believe we humans were meant to live that way.

In the land around Ucross, ten miles from the nearest town of Clearmont, there were Clear Creek, Piney Creek, and the Powder River. There were no large bodies of water, like the oceans or the Great Lakes.

"I miss water," Sharon Dynak, the executive director, told me. I suppose I would too if I lived there long enough, but in some odd way, those dry hills covered in fragrant sagebrush seemed to retain a memory of water that covered them eons ago.

In homeopathic medicine, where you treat a disease with a medicine similar to the malady—*homeo*, "same," and *pathic*, "illness"—remedies are made in the following way: A small quantity of the substance—say, cuttlefish ink for sepia—is infused into water. The medicine is "succussed," diluted further and further, until almost nothing remains of the substance but its memory in the water.

In our Westernized way of looking at the world, we don't think of things such as water or trees as having spirit or memory, but I believe it's possible that they do.

In Linda Hogan's novel *Solar Storms*, three women characters must travel through an area of dangerous rapids running through sheer canyon walls. In order for them to survive, one of them makes what the writer calls a bargain with water and then must give her life to fulfill the bargain.

I once heard a series of talks by Hershel Yolles, a traveling Hasidic *rebbe*, said to be a direct descendant of the Baal Shem Tov, founder of Hasidism. In one talk, Rabbi Yolles said that Mosherebbenu, his affectionate name for Moses, had made a mistake when he smote the Red Sea to part the water.

"He shouldn't have hit the water," the rebbe said, "because when he was a baby and his mother put him in the little boat, the water saved his life."

That was the first time I realized that traditional Judaism

might possibly have the same view of the earth as traditional Native American spirituality.

So, though very little water ran through the area where we were in Wyoming, the memory of water was all around us, and we moved about on the floor of the lake that had been there before.

———————

The Medicine Wheel, a series of rocks placed to form a circle with radiating spokes and cairns, or piles of rocks, placed strategically at primary directions, sits atop one of the Bighorn Mountains, ten thousand feet above sea level. You can go there only in late summer, because almost as soon as snow starts to fall, the National Park Service closes the road.

Like Bear Butte, it is a place for pilgrimage and vision quest for Native Americans, who have hung tobacco ties, sweetgrass braids, smudge sticks, and offerings on the fence surrounding the circle of rocks. It is one of many such circles that exist in the Americas.

Carbon dating of organic material left at campfires there has dated its construction at sometime between A.D. 1200 and 1700.

If it was built closer to 1200, its construction predated the introduction of the horse to the Americas. And the journey to the top of the mountain is so arduous, even by car, that you have to wonder how long it took to walk there. From the Park Service kiosk, it is a further mile-and-a-half walk, which was difficult for me to negotiate in the high mountain air.

Though the days previous to our trip had been in the eighties and nineties, there was snow on the ground at the Medicine Wheel, and I wore a hat, gloves, and scarf wrapped around my face to walk to the site. The sweater, hat, and scarf I wore were all things I had knitted. The sweater was the blue one I'd been knitting when my father died. It is by now stretched out and a little the worse for wear, but still comfortable, cozy, and warm.

The hat and the scarf were from my Colinette and pashmina binges, respectively. I've made the hat numerous times, with one skein of a thick yarn like Point Five, on size fifteen needles. The dye pattern in the yarn makes an interesting design on the hat.

I didn't find what I expected at the Medicine Wheel, but I was still glad I went; it could be my only chance this lifetime to get there.

I wanted to pray there. I was seeking answers to questions for myself, the same questions I've asked throughout this book. How do we live in the presence of death? What do I want from the rest of my life? How has my perspective been altered by the loss of my hopes and illusions about the saving power of romantic love?

———

I went to Wyoming in early September. One Sunday during my stay it rained. The thunder and lightning knocked out the signal on the satellite dish, just as another resident and I had settled down to watch *Sex and the City* deep in the boondocks, ten miles from Clearmont, the nearest town.

The next day revealed the sort of heart-stopping beauty I

sometimes see in the Bay Area after rain. The world had been washed clean. The greens were deeper and more varied in hue; the Bighorn Mountains rose bright blue in the distance; the sky was a sight you could long for your entire life.

Whatever power had brought me to that place, I counted myself forever in its debt.

I tried to stitch the beauty of Wyoming into the lipstick red of my needlepoint canvas. I knitted it into the many-hued oceanic blue of my silky lace shawl. All needlework to some extent functions as a repository of memory, of the events that were present surrounding their creation, what my daughter calls a tactile record.

I hoped to record in my stitches the nourishing silence of Wyoming, the unexpected sight of wildlife in the fields, the curious stares of white-tailed deer, the comical flutterings of a flock of wild turkeys. I relaxed into the luxury of having a separate studio dedicated to work and of being cared for while that work was performed.

I hoped to remember too that I had managed to get to Ucross, though it felt as though the dream had been lost in the sweeping away of everything but seemingly endless medical treatments with the cancer diagnosis. The treatments were over. I was healing from them. Eventually they passed, and I ended up going there despite them.

When I walked outside, I breathed the air of Wyoming, its empty spaces, restrained ocher palette, powerful winds, lunar shapes, the sound of shivering cottonwood leaves from what Indians called the rustling tree, the immanence of its landscape.

I wouldn't be there long enough, but I was satisfied to have been there at all. Like a trip I took to the Bear Paw Battlefield of Chief Joseph and the Nez Perce tribe's final standoff of the U.S. Army, it let me know that my intentions and longings could manifest as reality. I felt like the character in Faulkner's *Light in August* who constantly exclaims, "My, my. A body does get around."

I was happy such a place still existed, that the absolute inhospitability of its climate had kept it more or less unspoiled. That it could serve to invest our imaginations with spaciousness. To show what was possible in our world. In *The Solace of Open Spaces*, her book about Wyoming, Gretel Ehrlich writes that "closer to home we might also learn how to carry space inside ourselves in the effortless way we carry our skins. Space represents sanity, not a life purified, dull or 'spaced out' but one that might accommodate intelligently any idea or situation."

At Ucross, I felt not just the solace of open spaces but the desire to write again.

———

I had to get up at dawn to get to Wyoming. I was so anxious I wouldn't get up in time that I couldn't fall asleep. I think I had one hour of deep REM sleep, complete with a nightmare. I opened the door to my apartment, and two rough-looking people were ransacking it, waiting for me to get home. My body became drenched with fear. I let it happen because I'd been reading Pema Chodron. Go to the places that scare you, she said, transmitting the instructions of her Tibetan teacher, Chogyam Trungpa Rinpoche. Don't run from the feeling. So I let myself become drenched in fear, and then it was time to wake up.

Waiting for my plane at Great Lakes Aviation in the Denver airport, I noticed that Great Lakes also flew to Grand Island, Nebraska, where the sandhill cranes congregate each year. Now that I have heard the sound a few of these prehistoric creatures could make, I imagine the sound at Grand Island must be deafening.

Immediately after I got to Wyoming, I locked my keys in my studio, and my watch stopped. "You've stepped outside of time," said Sharon. At least I had remembered my binoculars, so I was able to see the cranes in the field.

"I'm not in my body," I told Sharon.

"Oh, the spirit lag," she said.

We had both read about the spirit lag in *Cowboys Are My Weakness* by Pam Houston. You fly somewhere on a jet plane, but all of you doesn't arrive at once. Your spirit travels at a different speed, so that you are already in Wyoming, say, while your spirit is still flying over Salt Lake City.

———

Wyoming wasn't so far from where I live, only a one-hour time difference. I was used to flying clear across the country, or at least to Minnesota, where there was a two-hour difference. When you go west from Minnesota through South Dakota, the time changes when you cross the Missouri River. I was reminded of how many trips I'd taken with Judycarol across the West. All in all, we've been on the road a lot.

The most haunting place we went was the Bear Paw Battlefield, sixteen miles south of the Canadian border, near Chinook, Montana. It was the site of Chief Joseph's last battle, the one where he was reported to have said, "From where this sun now stands I will fight no more forever." It represented the end of the line for the Nez Perce, after their famous flight from Idaho, through the Lolo Pass, across Flathead Indian territory in the Bitterroot Valley, through Yellowstone, and north to the Bear Paw Battlefield.

I had read about the Bear Paw Battlefield in the *New Yorker*, just after it had been designated a national park. The article's writer says that medicine people who came to consecrate the site reported they heard children crying. "It is cold and we have no blankets. The little children are freezing to death," Chief Joseph said there, after the Nez Perce had succeeded in holding off the U.S. cavalry over six days of heavy fighting.

I didn't hear children crying, but I was haunted by the windswept loneliness of the place. A pair of hawks circled over me as I walked, crying *kek kek, kek kek*, more, I think, because of the prairie dog town that spread out around me than for any spiritual purpose. What I really appreciated, though, was the way that I had wanted to come to this place and had succeeded in getting there. The manifestation of intention into action is a comparatively recent development in my life and one I count as almost a spiritual feat of attainment.

· I was alone as I walked through the fields, because Judycarol was resting her broken leg on the bench at the park entrance, where Indian visitors had placed sweetgrass braids, bundles of sage, prayer flags, and tobacco ties.

———————

There is an aliveness to the land in the sparsely populated West, the nearness of history, the seamless joining of the present with the past that matches the sense of time in the unconscious, the dream landscape where past, present, and future commingle all at once.

I felt the presence of the spirits of Indians who had roamed the Great Plains, as the buffalo that thundered over the ridges and hills left ghostly images of their sheer numbers on the land.

On one of our trips Judycarol and I had passed through Sheridan and Gillette and stopped in sight of the Bighorn Mountains. I didn't know then that I would end up spending time in that part of the country, becoming a high plains drifter.

I looked out the window of my writing studio at Ucross, a luxury I had rarely possessed in my grownup life, and realized how big a part the landscapes of the West had played in the territory of my imagination, my field of artistic inspiration, the way I had learned to think, feel, and operate in my later years. I realized the importance of place to me period. Place in fiction, place in dreams, place in reality, place in time.

I recalled one pilgrimage Judycarol and I undertook in the

early 1990s. I had found a yarn I liked called Rambolla. It was made from the fleece of Rambouillet sheep. (Coincidentally, my father had been in Rambouillet close to the end of World War II, after the Battle of the Bulge.) The yarn from the fleece of the Rambouillet sheep was as soft and wearable next to the skin as cotton. The label said the yarn was made in Roundup, Montana.

Judy and I drove north to Roundup, Montana. The way there was a stark landscape, like Navajo sheep ranches with nothing for miles but sagebrush and scrub. By this time we were tired of being in the car. Our backs ached, our butts ached, our minds ached from driving. Finally we arrived in Roundup. I was so sore from being in that car that I never wanted to get back in it again.

"I'll just stay here in Roundup," I said to Judycarol. "I'll rent a place, get a job on the newspaper, knit with nothing but Rambolla yarn." It matched the fantasy I once had of escaping from my troubled life in New York City by moving to Montana and becoming a waitress.

The address we had for Rambolla was a house in the middle of town, a very small town. No one was home at the address, though a bird flew around and around inside the screened-in porch. There was no sign whatever of a business. I tried the phone number. No answer. I asked around. Whatever brief flowering Rambolla yarn may have had as an entity seemed to have passed. No one I asked knew where there were any Rambouillet sheep to be found. People looked downright dumbfounded when I asked them.

The important thing for me, though, when I thought about it

afterward, was that I had been willing to undertake such a pilgrimage in search of a certain type of sheep and a certain brand of yarn. I still have my Rambolla sweater, in shades of burgundy and lavender. I never wear it, but I can't give it up. Years after I made it Kathryn Alexander, the great fiber artist, told me Rambouillet were known as "the cotton sheep."

After my trip to Roundup, I thought I might possibly become more interested in the origin of my knitting yarns, the processing of fleece "from sheep to shawl," as one knitting instructor puts it. It never happened. I never went deeper into spinning or dyeing, into carding or raising sheep. Various people have urged me to learn handspinning, but I always say it took me forty years to become a good knitter, and I don't have that kind of time to devote to spinning.

My trip to Roundup showed me in some curious way the depths of my love for knitting, the lengths to which I was willing to go.

Roundup was the polar opposite of the Montana landscape I found in early summer in the southeastern corner of the state, where the Powder River also flows, through lush green and rolling hills. This was along what Judycarol and I began to call the sage road. It was the road we took to a field where we gathered sage for smudging, a practice of purifying a person, place, or thing with fragrant smoke from sacred plants.

One day we were stopped by the side of the Little Powder River. Judycarol, who needed to sit on a stool to elevate her leg as she gathered sage from the edge of the road, was laying tobacco and gathering branches. I was standing by the river when a pair of pronghorn antelope came through the trees and stopped to watch me.

It was one of those intense interspecies encounters. I never know if they really happen or if they are the fruit of my overactive imagination, but the antelope and I stood stock-still and stared at one another for a good long time. Time out of time. I almost felt as though the soul of another entity or person were watching me through the limpid eyes of the antelope, and the encounter moved me profoundly.

At Ucross, in early September 2003, there was a similar landscape out the back window of my writing studio. Cottonwoods, aspens, box elders. Pronghorn weren't immediately evident, but I knew they were somewhere nearby. When I got the weather prediction for the Wyoming zip code where Ucross was, it said, "Visibility: unlimited."

I felt my father connected to that place, perhaps because Ricky had been at Ucross when our father began his final decline. One day we went "to town," into Sheridan, and I stopped by King's Saddlery, a legendary place in those parts. There was a museum behind King's Saddlery full of artifacts of the Old West and the Bozeman Trail, the trail through the Sioux hunting grounds that Crazy Horse so bitterly resented.

There were elk jackets and Indian beadwork in the museum, a sheep wagon outfitted with everything from pots and pans to an eiderdown comforter, with a life-size female mannequin holding a life-

size baby doll. There were big-game mounted heads and old-time ri-
fles. Most of all, there were bridles and saddles, rope and tack.

"My father would have loved this place," I thought.

In the front part of the museum, two genuine cowboys were
ordering tack. They wore boots, jeans, western shirts, and ten-gallon
hats. Ranching as a way of life is disappearing throughout the West,
but it persists in Wyoming. One early morning at Ucross I awoke to
hear, "Yip, yip, git along." Later that morning I saw that a herd of
black cattle had been moved to the field next to my studio.

Even more incredible than the cowboys, to my California eyes,
was the fact that they were smoking inside the store.

I was enthralled by the empty moonscapes of the Wyoming
landscape. It is my belief that we interact with place on some visceral
level. We absorb from the place where we stand, and send back to it,
some of what we are, in a circular loop of energy exchange.

I didn't know if I was brave enough to live in such an isolated
place. I'm a social animal and already missed the card games, friendship, and company I enjoyed back home. My Ucross residency was
a cross between heaven and solitary confinement. Though it seemed
much more like heaven when my brother was there to share it
with me.

I drew the Wyoming landscape into the needlework I'd
brought with me. Into the deep blue sea colors of my silk and wool
shawl, the vivid red of my needlepoint, the head of a fantasy creature from the Chinese New Year parade. Knitting is a part of nature.
Yarn comes from the earth as plants of flax or cotton, from the co-

coons of silkworms, the fleece of sheep. You sense your closeness to the animals as the fleece works through your hands.

There were visual artists in residence at Ucross who fixed the landscape on paper with watercolors or paint. Myself, I wrote and I stitched. Both anchored the sense of place in memory. And both gave something in return.

19. Lapidary Writing

I THINK OF MY WRITING AS SOMEWHAT INDISTINCT FROM my knitting or needlepoint, just another handcraft. The actual sentences that make up a piece must be formulated word by word with steady care, just as needlework must be patiently created stitch by stitch.

In order to succeed, a piece of writing must be steeped in place and imbued with culture. It has to occupy that exquisite balance point between the spot where each one of us is unique, a product of our own particular landscape and cultural heritage, and the place where we are all the same, the universal human experience.

There is very little that is totally original in writing. Nothing new under the sun. After all this time the mysteries of the human heart, of the spirit world, of mysticism, passion, love, and evil have been plumbed and deeply explored. Nevertheless, they have yet to be exhausted. Unlike the oceans, which seem so vast and limitless, they have been fished but not overfished.

The internal world is vast and limitless. It is the world of emptiness, not the emptiness of nothingness, but of the emptiness that can contain within itself everything there is. The fullness of emptiness, as it is sometimes called. It is a place of spaciousness, of vast horizons, of infinite interest to the questing mind.

Mysticism was another of those areas I thought I had discovered on my own, but it turns out to have been an interest of my father's as well. A longtime Freemason, a Past Master who attained the thirty-second degree, he preferred to have his mysticism firmly rooted in practical reality, the physical rules of building and architecture.

I cannot claim to know very much about Masonic secrets, though I remember my father studying hard to memorize the pages of text required to advance degrees. I know it sustained his lifetime devotion. I had the Masonic symbol engraved on his tombstone because it meant more to him than the religion he'd been born with.

Knitting has some similarities with architecture. Both involve complex mathematical calculations and need to follow ironclad rules of construction so as not to fall apart. Both must be done by hand and require the skillful work of craftspeople. A friend of mine, noting the columnar appearance of cables in my work, used to say I was "building a sweater."

Creativity is a mysterious and ultimately sacred pursuit. In order to have meaning, in my opinion, a work of art must contain within it the spark of divine nature that unites us with the Creator and all the Creation. Michael, my Rolfer, with whom I traded knitting for Rolfing sessions, said he liked to wear the things I had made, because I did "luminous knitting."

Luminous, full of light; numinous, full of soul. Two words close in sound, just shades away in meaning. I didn't demand the same degree of originality from myself in knitting that I did in writing, or the same degree of perfection. But I am the sort of person who needs to be doing two things at the same time anyway, and each one complemented the other.

I knitted to sink down into the place I wrote from, and knitted to bring myself back to the surface. I knitted while waiting for a piece of writing to shape itself in the depths of my unconscious. Contrary to what some people think, I don't believe writing comes from the cognitive part of the mind, the part that thinks thoughts and shapes spoken language. I write from a more invisible, almost nonverbal, musical center of mind. Writing is an alchemical process, wherein one attempts to transform the base metal of raw experience into gold.

I have sometimes had to play loud music to drown out the voices in my mind when I wrote, in order for the writing to emerge. And I think of it, like my knitting or needlepoint, as something that comes through my fingertips with the rhythmic tapping of the keys.

In order to write, I often need to put myself in what I call writing jail. Sometimes I need to do nothing for a whole day beforehand to descend into that space. I need to make myself a little crazy, take myself out of ordinary reality, build up the internal pressure until I can't do anything *but* write. Then I have to stay in the house until the writing is finished or spent for the day.

I have learned in writing what it means to stay out of my own way. In a certain sense, I have to step aside and become a conduit for the writing that is bursting to come out. I believe I write in something of an altered state. It feels as though an overabundance of electric current were flowing through me, not exactly a comfortable sensation, and I simply have to sit there and let it happen. Sometimes when I'm finished for the day, I think, "Having a wonderful time. Wish I were here."

I can't drive immediately after I've finished writing. I can't sleep. I am overamped for a number of hours. And when I become really deeply submerged in the writing process, such as in the final rewrite of a book that's been in process for years, I can't even have a normal conversation with another human being. Spoken words seem impossible at those times.

I don't think of myself as a poet, but I occasionally write a poem, usually when I have no choice but to write one. I think of the muse of poetry not as a sylphlike Botticellian creature, but as an angry old crone who takes hold of me and shakes me until I do what she wants me to do. Writing can be satisfying and fulfilling for me, and I can experience a great deal of peace when I finish it, but it is not an activity I would describe as pleasant or relaxing.

I think a lot of what people call writer's block is a misunder-standing of the creative process. There is a tremendous amount of internal processing, of gestation, that needs to take place before a piece of writing is ready to be born. "Emotion recollected in tranquillity" was how William Wordsworth described his poetry. The trick is that both the recollection and the tranquillity take time to come to fruition. Both involve labor, like the pains of childbirth, to come into the world.

When you travel by plane, you enter a sort of tunnel where time and distance have quite a different meaning. For me, when I write, I enter another sort of tunnel, a place of what another writer I know described as "ferocious concentration," where everything else is blocked out and nothing exists but the work.

Inspiration, in my experience, comes when you are actually working. It doesn't lift you off the couch to work. Sometimes there's nothing you can do but wait. Knitting is perfect for those times.

Rhythm is paramount in knitting. It is also paramount in writing. I prefer the sort of keyboard that makes a noise similar to a typewriter's, the clickety-clack of keys in rhythm while writing flows out of the hands. I used to write hundreds of drafts for the lead paragraphs of my magazine articles. I had to write until I got the internal rhythm right; then the rest of the piece could proceed.

Editing is where the lapidary part comes in, the patient crafting, the shaping and polishing, the cutting away of what is extraneous and distracting.

I am not talking here about digressions. In the work of Ian Frazier, one of my favorite writers, digressions can often be more interesting than the alleged subject of the work. For instance, in *Family*, his book about the history of his family, I was most taken by his descriptions of Stonewall Jackson, whose soldiers called him Old Blue Light because of his mystical bent, and of his dying words: "Let us cross over the river and rest under the shade of the trees."

Mythic accounts of dying and the afterlife often refer to the river Styx, where the dead are ferried to the other side. In the booklets that the hospice people left for my family when my father was dying, the journey of the dying person was also described as a sea voyage.

It did seem to me as my father lay unconscious in his hospice bed that he had some internal work to finish up, some preparations to be made. This was another time when all I could do was knit and wait.

The image of knitting, and the image of the knitting crone as a sort of sibyl or guardian of the underworld, has often been used in literature. The women in Dickens's *Tale of Two Cities* sat "knitting, knitting, counting dropping heads." In Joseph Conrad's *Heart of Darkness*, the traveler must obtain a ticket for passage down the river from the company office, where two women sit knitting black wool, bidding farewell to voyagers they may never see again.

There is something so archetypal and ancient about a woman knitting that writers have not been able to resist its allure as a symbolic representation.

Knitting is uniquely suited to times of life transitions, births and deaths, and passages in one's own evolution, such as pregnancy, illness, and menopause; it is a way to remain quiet and experience momentous events in the lives of those we love.

Both knitting and needlepoint have had the same result in terms of my writing. I stitch first thing when I wake up in the morning, and scribble whatever bubbles up from my mind—memories, insights, parts of songs—in a notebook I keep by my side. For me, the important thing is to keep my hands working so that words, stitching, memory flow.

———

I live a solitary life. It has occurred to me more than once that it is a life I have chosen for myself and something for which I perhaps longed through the whole of my childhood. It never occurred to anyone I knew to suggest that a grown woman might choose solitude as an option. You might end up an old maid because nobody wanted you or become a widow or divorcée through bad luck, but you would never make a conscious choice to be alone for work or spiritual fulfillment.

By nature, I am reclusive. I probably see more people than the average hermit does, but all outside my house. I like to have long hours of quiet and inactivity to dive down into my deepest thoughts, into the source of my writing. Not coincidentally, the source of my healing too.

I was not raised to live this life, but I embrace it. In some ways it is the very antithesis of the ideal for women that was glamorized in the 1950s. I was part of the generation of women who rejected that lot in life, threw it over for a full partnership with men, a full participation in the world.

Even in the women's movement, I went my own way. If I had ever suggested to the feminists I knew in the early 1970s that needlework might become a spiritual path, they would have laughed me out of a meeting. Now women younger than our first wave of the women's movement know that you can be both a feminist and an impassioned handcrafter; indeed the two are complementary.

I may have been a feminist in my beliefs and ideals, but for most of my life I looked for love to save me. Unconsciously I tried to live according to my mother's precepts and values. Now from the vantage point of middle age, I can see a whole string of romantic failures stretching behind me.

Yet it wasn't love that failed me, but my ideas about love. In the household where I grew up, there was one kind of love that was never mentioned, that was looked down upon, that was considered an unnatural emotion for a woman. That is the love that has ultimately saved me. Love of self. An ability to cultivate and obey your own deepest instincts. A fierce protection of your own time and desires.

I grew up in the 1950s. Its promise of better living through chemistry and plain hard work betrayed my father and destroyed his health. Its pesticides and environmental manipulations may ultimately cost me my life. But there are many ways I overcame my up-bringing. Openings through which I saw a faint light and somehow managed to break myself free.

———————

"Is this detachment or depression?" I asked Kathie Weston, the facilitator/therapist of our support group, on more than one occasion.

"It's too soon to tell," she answered. "You're still in the thick of the treatments."

I'm not in the thick of the treatments anymore. I'm engaged in the sorting out of what happened, mining for the gold of the experience, its meaning for the rest of my life.

There has been so far a kind of leveling. I love the people I love, but I know our relationships in our worldly form are impermanent. I accept that my father is gone. I think of him often, with gratitude and love. Sometimes when I go somewhere he would have liked, or watch a western on TV, I almost feel he is with me. But all the enthusiasms, preoccupations, and grudges of his life have vanished with his passing. *Poof.* Gone. Into thin air.

Partially because of that, I don't think what I do is so important anymore. One thing seems as good as another, and I've lost interest in some of what used to engage me.

Cancer reduced my life to stark simplicity. What was left after everything else was swept away was my love for the people with a claim on my heart, my respect for nature, and the healing power of craft: writing, knitting, needlepoint.

My artist-in-residence studio at Ucross held my computer, my manuscript in progress, my binoculars, my knitting—the ocean-colored lace shawl—and the dragon or lion face needlepoint.

The coffee table in front of the sofa was covered with bags of lustrous embroidery thread: shaded hues of yellow, green, purple, blue, and the vivid red that had drawn me to the design. My studio was a place to write and a place to stitch; both are intimate partners in the peculiar workings of my creativity.

These are the sources of my inspiration. I am uplifted by the sight of a raptor circling in the sky, by an unexpected encounter with an animal in the wild. I have found wordless communication with animals strangely fulfilling and am often surprised by the strength of love I feel for babies not related to me by friendship or blood.

I find, as I found as a child, a delicious pleasure in what I feel and fashion with my hands. The world of color, of fiber, of yarn and thread continues to enchant me.

I no longer ask myself why it is so absolutely soothing to me to ply a needle through fabric, in the same repetitive motion. The Mexican mural painter Diego Rivera said he painted because that was what he did. He was like a tree that bears a certain type of fruit; in his case the fruit was paintings.

I am a tree that bears needlework and writing. It's just what I do. I am comfortable with a needle and thread, needles and yarn, a pencil and a piece of paper. My body is at ease sitting cross-legged on the floor with knitting and pages spread out before me. I'm most myself, and at the same time most self-forgetful, while scribbling or stitching an item I hold in my hands.

I seem to have been born that way.

Epilogue:
My Daughter,
Knitting

April 2004

As I write this, in the spring of 2004, I'm back at Ucross, lucky enough to have another luxurious writing residency, a chance to complete a draft of this book. My brother, Ricky, is here too, working on an opera based on *The Grapes of Wrath.*

I'm still having problems with my health. I had about what seemed like five minutes after the breast cancer treatments ended to feel as if I might be a healthy person and return to a normal life. Then I was hit with a new crisis, more critical and dangerous than the one before.

I now have stage four cancer that has metastasized to my liver. The diagnosis was devastating, the new course of chemo only slightly less so.

In answer to the question of how this cancer

could have continued to grow undetected through adjuvant che-motherapy, the doctors offer one explanation: Different drugs are re-quired for both.

With my diagnosis comes a new level of empathy with my fa-ther, an inkling of how he must have felt as his time of death ap-proached, another opportunity to wonder how we live in the face of death.

"Don't forget this," Ricky said to me. "You're alive till you're dead." He has had close experience with this, having seen his former partner through death from AIDS. "Don't go getting all grandiose on me and thinking you know when you're going to die," he said. "Be-cause you don't."

Naturally, I'm knitting. I just gave Ricky a scarf I finished, of a lovely, hand-painted Mongolian cashmere I bought at Stitches last year, colored in rich autumnal shades: rust/burgundy, gold, and dove gray. He wore it this morning as he set off for the composer's log cabin to write music.

He calls it the Wyoming scarf, because it has absorbed so much of our time here together, as well as the constant wind that blows through this landscape in early spring. I knitted the scarf as part of my new guiding philosophy: Life is short; wear cashmere.

I joke although I am often distraught. When my doctors dis-covered the metastases, or "mets," as they like to call them, they looked at me with pity, as if I were already a goner.

But I'm the recipient of a brand-new drug with chemotherapy, a drug only recently approved by the Food and Drug Administration. It may turn out to be a miracle drug, as the protease inhibitors proved to be for AIDS patients. Or it may not. The chemotherapy may extend my life. Or it may not. At the moment it appears to be working.

I have a friend in the music business. In another time we would have been described as foxhole buddies. But we're really hell-hole buddies. We shared some dark days together in New York City. He invited me to his gig when he heard through the grapevine that I had cancer. "You know what?" he told me. "You were almost dead when I met you twenty-five years ago. You and I, we've lived on so much borrowed time we're on Shylock time now. And the vigorish is damn near unpayable."

Who really knows how much time we have left here on earth? "Let's face it, Sue," my mother says. "We're all here on a rental."

So we wait, as my daughter calls it, "in the Not Knowing." I watched her one night melting chocolate over an improvised double boiler in my kitchen, for a dessert she was creating, and thought: "This is an image I will take with me into the Beyond." My daughter, making dessert for her mother, not knowing how much of a future we have together.

I felt the same way about Ricky as I watched him play his music for the other Ucross residents, vibrating a difficult note through his body in a deeply felt song about our mother. "My mother is a singer; sing, Mama. Sing of what you gave up for the ring, Mama. Sing of how you gave up everything, Mama. Sing." I had to hold back tears as I fixed that picture too in the permanence of memory.

My life has taken on an exalted quality. Finally, I value deeply the time I have. I'm grateful for days out of the hospital, days without chemo. A day without a medical appointment feels like a holiday. I'm thankful to be alive. Especially during the times I feel good enough to write. I long to spend as much time as I can with my siblings, who seem more important to me than ever.

I am reminded of an interview I read with Robert Rauschenberg, the artist, now in his seventies and partially paralyzed. A *New York Times* reporter asked him why so many of his images had come from ordinary life.

"Most artists try to break your heart, or they accidentally break their own hearts," said Rauschenberg. "But I find the quietness in the ordinary much more satisfying."

That has become my sustenance: the quietness in the ordinary. I have moments of sheer happiness sometimes, when nothing particularly memorable is happening. These moments of joy rise from nowhere and sweep over me like a gentle tide. I have them at the ocean, sometimes just being near the ocean, breathing what Marilyn's mother always exclaimed about on Cape Cod: *die Luft, die Luft.*

My daughter has begun knitting. When I received my diagnosis, I told her she had better learn to knit so I could teach her what I knew before it was too late. But she had already determined to do that herself. Her friend in Portland taught her to knit in the American style, where you "throw" the yarn instead of picking it off the opposite needle.

Shuna told me she was uncomfortable knitting that way. Then she thought: "Wait a minute. Haven't I seen my mom do *this*?" Here she mimed winding yarn around her finger in a motion she must have seen me do a million, possibly a trillion, times before. Once she switched to knitting continental, the way I knit, she was perfectly comfortable and has since shown a lot of natural ability.

Let a thousand knitters bloom!

Maybe when my time comes, my daughter will help to knit me out of this world.

My sister Lorraine too has rediscovered knitting. The bug has bitten her badly. Now, like me, she spends all her money on yarn.

She made me a ruby red scarf of lush Touch Me, a rich chenille yarn that shines like panne velvet. She calls me for advice and to share our enthusiasm for the beauty of a certain yarn, the pure pleasure of knitting.

When I think about leaving a legacy, as my father did near the end of his life, I'm happy I've written articles and books. But I also think of my knitting and needlepoint. I've tried to give most of the people who are close to me something I've made with my hands. I imagine them in shawls or hats or sweaters I have made, warmed by the crafts that buoyed me through difficult times in my life.

Lorraine sent me a book about the Lakota medicine man Frank Fools Crow. A bust of Fools Crow stands at the foot of Bear Butte, a place I've often traveled for healing. Like the Powder River country, Bear Butte was a place loved by Crazy Horse.

In *Fools Crow: Wisdom and Power*, the book Lorraine sent me,

Fools Crow told the writer Thomas E. Mails, "Not everyone can be cured, but everyone can be healed."

This is an important distinction. Curing is a matter of the body only, healing a matter of the heart, spirit, and soul. According to Fools Crow, healing is "reaching peace, which [is] freedom from fear."

Whether or not I live or die, I've experienced in my life a tremendous healing. The stitches I've made with my hands, one following another, have carried me to a peaceful landscape within, a place of spacious presence and luminous hope.

The landscapes I've visited in the outer world have given me more than I can express in words, a kind of rapture, maybe, a steady appreciation for the beauty and wonder of Creation, for everything created, including myself.

My days have been sweetened by the love of friends, the bonds of family, the kindness, intimacy, and even harsh pain brought by lovers.

I'm becoming somewhat detached from worldly care, though this is not always true. Once you've "been given your pink slip," as my friend Erica Apollo puts it, everything takes on a different cast. I can't claim to have become totally detached or to possess the sort of equanimity I believe will be needed to face the end with grace. I'm still in a process that is by turns agonizing, rageful, hopeful, unconscious, in denial, filled with false hope, or possibly true.

I might live for a while, or maybe not. Nobody knows for sure. But I do have one possible answer to the question I have posed in this book: How do we live in the presence of death? I asked my friend Jimmy Hanlon, who has lived for over twenty-five years with the AIDS virus, uncertain whether he had a future. He gave me the same answer as Kathie Weston, whose decades of spiritual study have led her to a strong belief in the power of being here now.

Do whatever it is you're doing. Let your mind roam free.

Now slowly, gently, bring yourself back to the present moment.

Sink down deeply into where you are right now, into the eternal present.

This moment is all there is. And it's enough.

SHEILA WOLFF

SUSAN GORDON LYDON is the author of *Take the Long Way Home: Memoirs of a Survivor* and *The Knitting Sutra: Craft as a Spiritual Practice*. She has written for numerous magazines, including the *New York Times Magazine*, *Ms.*, *Interweave Knits*, and *Rolling Stone*, which she helped found. She has also taught knitting retreats at the Esalen Institute in Big Sur, California. Lydon lives in the San Francisco Bay Area.